R0020803494

CHICAGO PUBLIC LIBRARY
HAROLD WASHINGTON LIBRARY CENTER

R0020803494

BUSINESS/SCIENCE/TECHNOLOGY DIVISION
CHICAGO PUBLIC LIBRARY
400 SOUTH STATE STREET
CHICAGO, IL 60605

ALL ABOARD!

The railroad trains that built America

by Mary Elting

FOUR WINDS PRESS/NEW YORK

625.1009
EL83a
cop.2
TECH.

Also by Mary Elting (with Franklin Folsom):
IF YOU LIVED IN THE DAYS OF THE WILD MAMMOTH HUNTERS

THE CHICAGO PUBLIC LIBRARY

JUL 21 '71   B

Published by Four Winds Press
A Division of Scholastic Magazines, Inc., New York, N.Y.
Copyright 1951 by Franklin Watts, Inc.
Revised edition copyright © 1969 by Mary Elting
All Rights Reserved
Printed in the United States of America

Library of Congress Catalogue Card Number: 78-124183

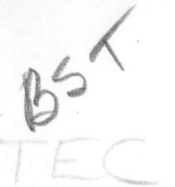

R00208803494

BUSINESS/SCIENCE/TECHNOLOGY DIVISION
CHICAGO PUBLIC LIBRARY
400 SOUTH STATE STREET
CHICAGO, IL 60605

They looked like huge monsters. They belched sparks and smoke, ran off the rails, and sometimes even exploded. But everyone wanted to ride behind the fast, new steam locomotives.

Soon railroads connected the big eastern cities, and a mad race was on to link them with the Far West. As western rail crews blasted a way east through the high mountains, work gangs from the East laid track westward. Each rail crew strove to lay the most track.

They met in Utah, on May 10, 1869. As the last spike—the Golden Spike—was driven in, everybody cheered. The race to span a continent was won.

This is the story of those exciting dangerous days—the days of the steam trains—when fortunes were made and lost, and men worked and died to build America's railroads.

Mary Elting
Roosevelt, New Jersey

CALOVAO' I Aoas4
ARS BOOK STOC SLPCS OR
-83557 MANN OCL'TO
GRAMAESTAGOASTZSTFGRAM4F16 DIAT2C3

CONTENTS

The Best Friend of Charleston. CULVER PICTURES

1

When They Were Very New

"Hold onto your hats!" shouted the passengers. It was 1831, and a small, noisy locomotive named the *Best Friend of Charleston* was giving Americans their first real train ride.

The tiny engine wheezed and rattled over six miles of track in South Carolina. It pulled a flatcar, on which a cannon was mounted, and some open carriages filled with men, women, and children. These brave passengers loved every jerk and jolt of the trip. Ladies in frilly bonnets and men wearing black stovepipe hats fanned away the smoke and sparks that flew from the engine. The boys and girls cheered at every blast from the cannon, which had been loaned by the army for this special trip. The soldiers riding with it on the flatcar fired joyful salutes all along the way.

More smoke—more sparks—and the locomotive picked up speed. Now it was traveling ten, fifteen, eighteen, twenty-one miles an hour!

A crowded and uncomfortable stagecoach. The driver made many stops to hitch fresh teams of horses to the stage. BROWN BROTHERS

Oliver Evans' invention was called Orukter Amphibole. It was the first wheeled, steam-driven vehicle ever to run in America. Its rear paddle drove it in water. BROWN BROTHERS

Twenty-one miles an hour—it was marvelous, unbelievable! In 1831, people still traveled by wagon or stagecoach, and a fifty-mile journey took at least two days. Roads—and there were few—were terrible. When it rained, wheels stuck hub-deep in mud. When the roads dried, wheels cracked and broke in the hardened, treacherous ruts. Passengers in the crowded stage-coaches got so bounced and bruised that most men chose to travel on horseback whenever they could.

For every person who had a chance to ride, there were dozens who had to walk. And walk they did— sometimes hundreds of miles. Before a railroad to the West was built, one man pushed a wheelbarrow filled with his belongings all the way from Illinois to the Great Salt Lake, more than a thousand miles.

A better way to travel was what everyone needed, and inventors had been trying for a long time to find one. How could they build a machine to make transportation quicker and easier? What about using a steam engine?

For more than a hundred years steam engines had pumped water out of coal mines. Could such engines also turn a paddle wheel—or even the wheels of a carriage? Oliver Evans, a nineteen-year-old American boy, thought so, and in the summer of 1804 he proved it. He built a new kind of steam engine and installed it in a combination boat and wagon. This strange amphibious craft steamed up the river to Philadelphia, crawled out onto land, and rumbled on wheels through the city streets!

The steam carriage worked. But what a monster it was! Its fifteen tons of machinery could turn the wheels only three miles an hour on the paved cobblestone streets. Most American roads were unpaved and often muddy, and such a heavy carriage would simply get stuck.

Other men were working on other ideas to make travel easier. In one city, wooden rails were laid for the horse-drawn streetcars, and wooden tracks on a few country roads kept wagon wheels from sinking into the mud. These rail-roads, everyone agreed, were a great improvement. But even on tracks, horse-drawn vehicles were slow and not very practical.

Finally, the ideas of rails and steam-driven vehicles came together. America's first locomotive appeared in 1825. It ran around a circular track in the builder's back yard. Four years later a small steam locomotive, which had been built in England, made a three-mile run on tracks in Pennsylvania. Then in 1830 a little American engine called the *Tom Thumb* proved it could puff along the rails at eighteen miles an hour.

Now, in 1831, the *Best Friend of Charleston* in South Carolina had actually pulled passenger cars at twenty-one miles an hour! No wonder people cheered and celebrated. For the first time in America, a fast, new means of travel was possible. People everywhere talked about the amazing steam engine and its possibilities. They found the idea of train travel as exciting as space travel is to us today. The whole country began to want railroads. And it didn't have long to wait.

Builders laid tracks in New Jersey, in Pennsylvania, and in New York. The excitement grew as trains started to roll. At every station, men flocked around to watch, hoping for a chance to drive the new steam locomotives, or to heave wood into the fireboxes that made the steam. Many a young farmer who rode into town just to see what a train looked like took his horse home and returned to spend the rest of his life working for the railroads.

Whenever a new stretch of track was finished, everyone came from miles around to celebrate. The

America's first locomotive ran round and round on a circular track.
STEVENS INSTITUTE OF TECHNOLOGY LIBRARY

*Even though the Tom Thumb ran faster than this horse-drawn car,
the horse won the race because the locomotive broke down.*
BROWN BROTHERS

People came from miles around to see the steam train. Carriages, buggies, stagecoaches, and wagons waited at the station when the train pulled in.
METROPOLITAN MUSEUM OF ART, BEQUEST OF MOSES TANENBAUM, 1937

Because boilers in those days often exploded, cars were loaded with bales of cotton to protect the passengers. SOUTHERN RAILWAY COMPANY

stations were decorated with flowers. The crowd would whoop and cheer while soldiers and cavalrymen paraded and church bells rang. Then there were solemn ceremonies and speeches, and the grand opening almost always ended with fireworks at night.

People loved the sight and sound of a train, and they had endless questions to ask.

Could a locomotive go uphill? In the beginning, railroad tracks were laid on flat ground, and some men argued that an engine would never be able to pull a train up a slope. The slippery wheels, they said, would just spin round and round on the smooth rails. Yet when the railroad builders went ahead and laid tracks on hillsides, they found that a locomotive really could haul a train up a gentle slope.

Could trains run in winter? Snow did block the tracks. To solve this problem, railroaders attached V-shaped metal plates to the front of a locomotive and made a snow plow that cleared the tracks.

How fast could a locomotive go? One engineer said, "A mile a minute."

"Rubbish!" said those who heard him.

In 1848 an engine called the *Antelope* ran twenty-six miles in twenty-six minutes, pulling one small coach. The passengers were so frightened that they lay down on the floor, closed their eyes, and prayed.

Was it safe to ride on a train? Not really, but most people didn't think about the dangers. Often engines or even whole trains would run off the track and the

wooden carriages would catch fire. Passengers were lucky if they escaped with only a scare.

The early locomotives themselves were dangerous. Their power came from steam boilers. To make steam, a fireman shoved wood into the firebox that was attached to the boiler. He kept the flames blazing high. Live sparks poured from the smokestack along with smoke. A passenger who dozed in the open car might wake up to find his clothes on fire.

Sometimes the steam boilers exploded. Of course, the boiler always had a safety valve, which opened automatically to let out the extra steam. If firemen didn't realize how important the safety device was, however, it too could be dangerous. One fireman who couldn't stand the constant hiss of escaping steam from the safety valve fastened it down tight. That ended the hissing sound. But a few minutes later the boiler blew up, and ended the locomotive and fireman as well.

There were other dangers. Floods washed away whole sections of rail. Bridges collapsed. Sometimes a wagon driver would race a locomotive to the crossing. When the driver didn't get across the tracks in time, he and the train's crew and passengers would lose their lives in the crash of train and wagon. Cattle wandered onto the tracks. To push them off and prevent derailing, a cowcatcher was attached to the front of the locomotive.

Would the train be on time? In the early days of railroading, a traveler needed courage. He needed patience, too. His train might be hours late and there would always be more delay when it came to one of the big rivers, such as the Hudson. The passenger would have to get out, take a boat or ferry across the water, and board another train. (There were no tunnels or long bridges in those days.) Each railroad company

The wedge-shaped cowcatcher attached to the engine pushed wandering animals out of the train's path. P.&P.R.R.

had its own station in the larger towns and cities, and passengers making a long trip usually had to change from one railroad line to another in each city they came to. On a five-hundred-mile journey, which could easily take four days, they might have to ride on twelve different railroads.

Everything about railroading was uncertain—it was also full of wonderful adventure. Those noisy, dangerous trains carried people farther and faster than they had ever gone before. Families could visit distant friends, or see the sights, or move to new places. And soon dozens of new inventions began to make railroad travel easier and a little safer.

Engineers often decorated their headlights with deer antlers or even a deer's head. UNION PACIFIC RAILROAD MUSEUM COLLECTION

**Inventions
Small and Large**

The more Americans traveled by rail, the more problems there were to be solved.

At first the trains ran only in daytime. But soon they were carrying more passengers and freight than they could manage between dawn and dusk. Why couldn't trains run at night? They could have—if the engineers had been able to see the tracks. How could the tracks be lighted?

A young railroader named Horatio Allen had one solution: cover a wooden flatcar with a thick bed of sand. Then make a bright fire of pine wood on the sand and push the flatcar ahead of the train.

Many a locomotive went through the night lighted in this way. Since an open bonfire didn't really light up the tracks ahead very well, some kind of headlight was needed. The first one was just a candle set inside a glass protector that kept the wind from blowing out the flame. Behind the candle, a shiny metal reflector helped to make the light brighter.

STOP   **ALL RIGHT**   **SLOW**

Signals from a book of railroad rules in 1855.

Next came the oil headlamps, which gave more light. The lamps burned whale oil, which was not very expensive at first. Then the oil suppliers decided to raise prices. By the 1840's they were charging so much that railroad owners said the old candle headlights might have to be used again.

Just in time a lamp was invented which burned a new kind of inexpensive fuel called kerosene. A big kerosene lamp made a wonderful headlight. Now engineers could really see through the darkness ahead of the locomotive.

Someday railroaders would have electric headlights, but for that important invention they would have to wait until 1881.

Good train wheels were just as important as lights. Wheels had to turn easily, and that meant they had to be greased—just like wagon wheels. A wagon driver could always tell when a wheel needed greasing—it squeaked. The trouble was that a railroad train rolled

along with such a clatter that nobody could hear a squeaking wheel.

In addition, railroad cars traveled at higher speeds than wagons, and the increased friction of the fast-moving wheels heated the metal axles and melted away the grease. Without grease the metal axle would wear down and eventually break. A broken axle could wreck a whole train.

Again it was a railroader who solved the problem by inventing a special kind of axle. Around each end of this axle he put a container called a *journal box*. The journal boxes held wads of string soaked in oil and packed close around the axle tips. As long as oil remained in the string, the wheels turned smoothly. When the oil was used up, the axle grew hotter, and heat made the string smoulder and smoke.

A smoking journal box warned the train's crew. They called it a *hotbox* or a *stinker*, and whenever anyone saw the telltale smoke, he signaled for the engineer to stop the train immediately. Then new oily string was packed into the journal box, and the train could go on.

The journal box turned out to be one of the most important of all railroad inventions. Whenever two trains passed, the crew of each one always looked to see if the other had a "stinker." Stationmasters watched for smoking hotboxes, and so did the men who kept the track repaired. They stopped work as the train ran by and gave it what they called a "running inspection." Anyone who saw smoke would hold his nose with one hand and raise the the other above his head. This special signal told the engineer to stop the train at once.

People who lived along the track watched out for hotboxes and for other dangers, too. In those days everyone within miles of a railroad knew just when the trains were scheduled to run. They waited for the engine's

Torpedo
ILLINOIS CENTRAL RAILROAD

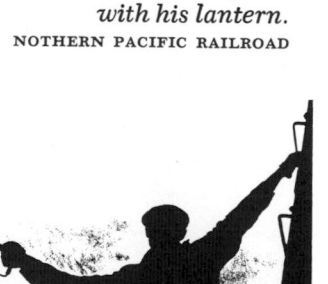

A brakeman signals with his lantern.
NOTHERN PACIFIC RAILROAD

whistle and worried when it did not come on time. After a storm they often hurried to find out whether a bridge or a section of track had been washed away. If it had, they knew what to do: snatch up something red and wave it at the engineer. Since bright red underwear was in fashion then, it was a likely thing to use in flagging down a train. Railroaders said it saved many a life.

Red flags and red lights have become standard railroad danger signals because they are easy to see at a distance. Through the years other signals were developed, too. Especially important were those which kept one train from plowing into another that was stalled on the tracks.

Whenever an engineer had to stop unexpectedly, the rear brakeman (also called the flagman) would leap off the train and run back for about half a mile along the track. There he would strap onto the rail something that looked like a tiny gray pillow. It was a small torpedo that exploded loudly when the wheel of a locomotive went over it. Exploding torpedoes warned the engineer in the oncoming train: Stop immediately!

The flagman also carried *fusees* and set them into the ground beside the rails. A fusee looked like a giant firecracker which produced a shower of glowing red sparks when it was lit. The sparks were cool, so they could not cause a fire, but they could be seen a long way off.

For extra protection in daytime the flagman carried a red flag to wave. At night he waved a lantern to signal that his train was stalled on the track ahead.

When the rear flagman ran out with his safety devices, the head brakeman sprinted forward to protect the front of the train. Then, as soon as the emergency was over, the engineer blew the whistle to call both flagmen in.

Danger ahead! This locomotive just struck a torpedo that warns the engineer to stop immediately. CULVER PICTURES

Torpedoes, fusees, flags, and lanterns are still used as safety devices, although today there is also much automatic safety equipment that works electronically. If these should fail for some reason, the simple torpedoes, fusees, flags, and lanterns are used just as they were long ago.

Many railroads had good iron wheels before they had good iron rails. In the beginning, rails where made of wood with strips of iron pegged along the top. Every passing train shook the rails and loosened the pegs a little. Finally the metal strips would break loose, curl up and strike unexpectedly through the floors of the cars, sometimes injuring the passengers. These loosened strips were called "snakeheads" because they were as dangerous as rattlesnakes.

In the early days, short lengths of rail were laid by hand.
BETTMANN ARCHIVE

Today, rails are sometimes attached to ties before they reach the roadbed. Machines lift sections of track into place.
LOUISVILLE & NASHVILLE RAILROAD

Even though solid iron rails made a much safer track, at first no factory in the United States had the equipment to shape solid rails. Until 1844 rails had to be bought in England and carried across the ocean in sailing vessels. Solid rails were, therefore, expensive— too expensive, some railroad builders insisted, and for years they kept many trains running over the dangerous wooden rails.

Some of the earliest solid rails were fastened to stone blocks sunk in the ground. In spite of their weight, the blocks did not make a level rail bed. In winter the earth around the blocks froze, then thawed, and froze again. Each time this happened, the frost-swollen earth would heave the blocks and push the rails out of line.

How could the tracks be laid so that they would stay in line?

Railroaders finally came up with an idea. They fastened rails to slabs of wood laid crosswise on the ground. The wooden slabs, called *crossties,* or simply *ties,* rested on a bed of cinders or crushed stone. These hard little particles didn't pack together tightly, and water would drain away from them before it could freeze. This method of laying track worked so well that railroads have been using it ever since.

Solid iron rails, spiked to wooden ties, had their hazards also. If a solid rail was imperfect, it cracked and broke under the weight of trains. Repair men kept a constant watch for rail breaks. So did the people who walked along the tracks.

Once a hobo in Connecticut discovered a broken rail. Since he had often stolen rides on this very railroad, he was familiar with the schedule, and he knew that a passenger train would be along any minute. If he raced to meet it, perhaps he could stop the train before it was thrown from the track.

Off he went. When the locomotive appeared in the distance, the hobo began waving his red bandana. The engineer saw him, slowed down, and stopped the train in time.

Passengers jumped off to see what had happened. When the engineer thanked the hobo, one passenger called out, "Give him a reward!"

The hobo said "No." He figured he had just about paid the railroad for all the free rides he had taken—and for those he still intended to take.

Rails could break, and they could also become very slippery. On a rail made slick by ice or oil, locomotive wheels would turn round and round without pulling the train forward.

In 1836, the year of the great grasshopper plague in Pennsylvania, a railroader used the first good anti-slipping device. One summer day millions of grasshoppers swarmed across the rails. When a train ran over them, the squashed grasshoppers made the track as slick as if it had been oiled. The locomotive barely moved, although its wheels were turning at full speed. At last one of the crew hopped out and shoveled *sand* onto the rails. The engine moved ahead!

The news about the sand spread quickly. Engineers began to carry along a bucket of sand to use on wet or icy tracks. Then the builders of locomotives heard of the idea. Soon all of their engines were equipped with a sand dome—a special container built on top of the locomotive near the smokestack. Now, instead of stopping to shovel sand onto the tracks, engineers could squirt it out through pipes which opened in front of the wheels. A squirt or two of sand also made it easier for a locomotive to pull a heavy train up a steep slope. To this day, locomotive engineers still use sand. No one has ever thought of a better remedy for slick rails.

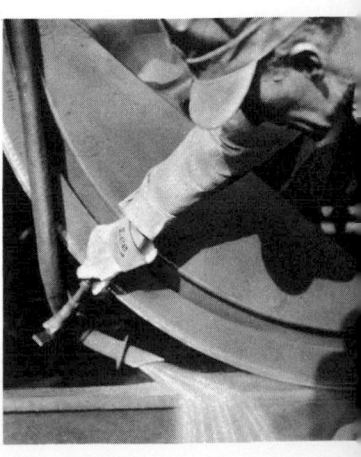

Sand and fuel for modern diesels are stored beside the track.
An engineer checks to make sure that an even stream of sand flows
in front of the wheels. RAILROAD MAGAZINE

The cars needed many improvements too. In 1836, passenger trains were far from comfortable. Soon, however, roomy cars with windows replaced the small open carriages. In cold weather travelers could now enjoy the warmth of a stove at one end of each car.

Locomotives that pulled passenger trains continued to burn wood. By this time good coal-burning locomotives had been invented, but they were unpopular with passengers who complained indignantly about the cinders and soot that poured from the smokestacks. As a result, coal-burners were used chiefly to haul freight. Many railroads kept their wood-burning passenger locomotives until long after the Civil War.

Even before the Civil War, locomotives looked very different from the first little steam engines. They were bigger, stronger—and much more handsome. By 1850 locomotives were pulling a dozen cars, fully loaded. Often gay colors, or even specially painted pictures, decorated both the locomotive and the tender—the car that carried the wood or coal.

In good weather and bad, the engineer and the fireman on the early locomotives stood and worked on an

The Pioneer, a famous locomotive, was in working order from 1848 to 1936. CHICAGO AND NORTH WESTERN RAILWAY

Engineers were proud of their locomotives. Many engines and tenders displayed polished brass, paintings, fancy lettering, and colorful decorations. COVERDALE & COLPITTS COLLECTION

open platform. There was a certain safety in this—when they saw trouble coming, they could easily jump off. That was the only advantage, however, and the men welcomed the first enclosed cabs. Now the engineer was protected, and the fireman, too, could take shelter in the cab when he wasn't heaving fuel into the firebox.

The fireman on a coal-burner had to be expert at his job. It was not easy to aim and spread the coal so that it would burn just right. If he shoveled in too much coal, the fire would die down for a time, and the engineer would yell for more steam. Too hot a fire would send steam hissing out through the safety valve. Then the engineer would lecture him for wasting fuel. Just the same, the fireman on a locomotive wouldn't have traded jobs with anybody—except the engineer!

By 1850 there were dozens of railroads and 9,000 miles of track in the United States, and still the building went on. The fireman's chances to drive the locomotive got better every year!

All the railroad lines operating in the United States in 1850. There were 9,021 miles of track, mostly in the northeastern area.
ASSOCIATION OF AMERICAN RAILROADS

By 1860 it was possible to travel by rail from the Hudson River to the Mississippi. As the railroads grew, their owners had more and more complicated problems to solve. The solutions became more and more ingenious.

For example, how could trains traveling in opposite directions use the same track without crashing into one another?

The answer was to build special *sidetracks* where one train could turn off to let another train pass. The system worked well—until engineers began racing to see which one could force the other to use the turnout. Sometimes these races ended in collisions.

How could the sidetracks be made safer? The manager of the railroad had to make up a schedule—a plan for the meeting and passing of trains at certain times and places. Strict rules now told each engineer when he had to pull his train onto the sidetrack and when he could go straight through on the main line.

If all the engineers had been able to run on schedule, this solution would have worked. But trains were often delayed for unscheduled reasons. Sometimes a herd of cows would stand in the middle of the track until the fireman chased them off. The water in the engine might boil away too fast, and the fireman would have to fill the boiler from the nearest stream, often with the help of the passengers. In the meantime, other trains along the line had to stop and wait on the sidetracks. An engineer didn't dare go forward for fear he would run head on into the late train. These delays were a terrible nuisance until a man named Charles Minot lost his temper and found a solution to the problem.

Minot was superintendent of the New York & Erie Rail Road, and he often made trips on his own trains. One day in 1851 he found himself in a car that had to wait for a long time on a sidetrack at a scheduled stop. Other passengers hopped out and walked up and down the station platform. Charles Minot sat and fumed.

Finally he could stand it no longer. He rushed into the station and sent a telegram to the next station along the line: Had the oncoming train arrived yet? In a few minutes he had an answer. The train had not yet reached that station. The track ahead was clear.

Minot sent another telegram, instructing the station agent to hold the late train on a sidetrack when it arrived. Then Minot rushed back to his train and told the engineer to pull out.

The engineer refused. The rules said he must wait, and wait he would.

Minot was stubborn. He climbed into the locomotive, took the throttle, and ran the train himself.

At the next station he telegraphed ahead again. Again it was safe to go on. Triumphantly Minot brought his train to its destination. He had solved a great prob-

In the stationmaster's office, the telegraph operator sent and received messages with the telegraph key.
SHELBURNE MUSEUM, SHELBURNE, VT.

lem. From then on, engineers didn't have to rely on schedules alone. They could get their orders by telegraph, too.

The telegraph was almost as exciting an invention as the locomotive. People called it the Lightning Wire, because electric current carried the message over wires from one station to another.

News came over the Lightning Wire, too. Now people didn't have to wait for days or weeks to find out who had won a battle or how an election had turned out. Sometimes, in the middle of an important story, the telegraph operator would say, "That's all. Quitting time." Then everyone who wanted to hear the rest of the news would have to put a nickel or a dime into a hat to pay the operator for working overtime.

Telegraph key
BROWN BROTHERS

When a telegraph operator was receiving a message, he listened to a series of clicks that came from a little brass button on his desk in the railroad station. The button was moved up and down by electric current, its clicks spelling out words in Morse code. A short click stood for the letter *e;* a long one stood for *t;* a long and a short for *n;* and so on.

To send a message, the operator tapped that same button, which he called the *bug*. Letter by letter he spelled the words in clicks. Miles away, on another operator's desk, another bug clicked out the message exactly as he had sent it. As an operator listened, he spelled the words in his head and wrote them down by hand on thin paper called *flimsy*. A skilled telegraph operator could write as fast as the words came over the wire.

When an operator received train orders, he always wrote out two copies of it on flimsy, one for the conductor, the other for the engineer. The two railroaders could then check with each other and make sure they had understood the orders.

What if a train wasn't scheduled to stop at a station? How could the men get their flimsies? At such a station the operator had to "hoop the orders up," that is, he fastened the flimsies to hoops and stood with them beside the tracks. The engineer grabbed one hoop and the conductor grabbed another as they leaned from the moving train. Then they quickly unfastened the flimsies and dropped the hoops beside the track to be picked up.

Train orders are still called flimsies, and they are still hooped up along some stretches of road. More often than not, the hoop is now a holder on a slender pole that stands beside the track. Only a few operators, however, still know how to use Morse code. Today, most telegraph messages are typewritten on a teletype machine.

The modern telegraph operator still hoops up flimsies which the rear conductor grabs as the train goes by.

PHOTOGRAPHER: WM. C. TAYLOR, LOUISVILLE & NASHVILLE RAILROAD

The telegraph was splendid for sending messages a long distance. But what about short distances—from the locomotive to the back of the train, for example? How could the engineer tell the conductor he was going to start or stop or back up? The answer was: The engineer could blow a whistle.

No one knows the name of the engineer who first had the idea of using the steam from the boiler to make a loud, musical sound in a length of pipe. By 1837 locomotive builders had adopted the idea and were installing steam whistles on the new engines.

The engineers discovered to their delight that they could do all kinds of things on their whistles. One found his whistle set up such strong vibrations that he could blow out kerosene lights as he went past the stations. Another put together a device on which he could blow tunes. This was called *quilling*. Many an engineer could make the whistle laugh or chuckle, wail like a wildcat, sing like a bird, or even play *Home Sweet Home*.

The real purpose of the whistle was to give signals or warnings. Three toots meant that the train, if it were standing still, would back up. If it were running, three toots meant it would stop at the next station. Two long toots, then a short and a long, warned everyone—including drivers of wagons—that the train was approaching a road crossing. Before long more than a dozen toot-signals were worked out and written down in the official rule book that all railroads used.

As more trains were put into operation, there were other problems to solve. One concerned the crews that ran the trains.

On a locomotive the engineer and fireman had shelter in the locomotive cab. On a passenger train the conductor and brakeman rode in the cars. Where could the conductors and brakemen on freight trains ride? In the caboose.

Inside the modern caboose, a conductor can talk by radiotelephone to the engineer at the head of the train. SANTA FE RAILWAY

Although nobody knows which railroad first built a caboose—a small special car, usually painted red, and always the last car in the train—by 1865 freight crews on the road were making the caboose their home. There they rested in bunks or cooked meals on the coal stove, and many a railroader grew famous for his cooking.

Railroad rules said that the only passengers allowed to ride with crew members in the caboose were cattlemen and sheepmen and then only when the train was carrying their animals to market. Sometimes, however, a crew would decide that the rules didn't apply to some very special person. One such person was Abraham Lincoln. When he was a young lawyer in Illinois, Lincoln had very little money to buy tickets on trains.

Top : An old-time wooden red caboose built for the Rock Island Railroad Line. PHOTOGRAPHER : F. WESLEY KRAMBECK, RAILROAD MAGAZINE

Bottom : A Long Island Rail Road caboose. Instead of the cupola, some modern cabooses have a bay window. RON ZIEL

On his way from one courthouse to another, he was often made welcome in the caboose.

After the Civil War, car builders began to put cupolas on top of cabooses. A cupola was a tiny tower room with windows all around in which a crew member could sit and keep an eye on the whole train ahead.

Railroaders nicknamed the cupola the *cockloft*. They gave the caboose many nicknames—*crib, monkey house, cage, doghouse, buggy, glory wagon, way car, crumb box,* or—more often—*the crummy.*

Today a caboose may have a bay window instead of a cupola, and it may be orange or green instead of red. But it is still called the crummy and probably will be for a long time to come.

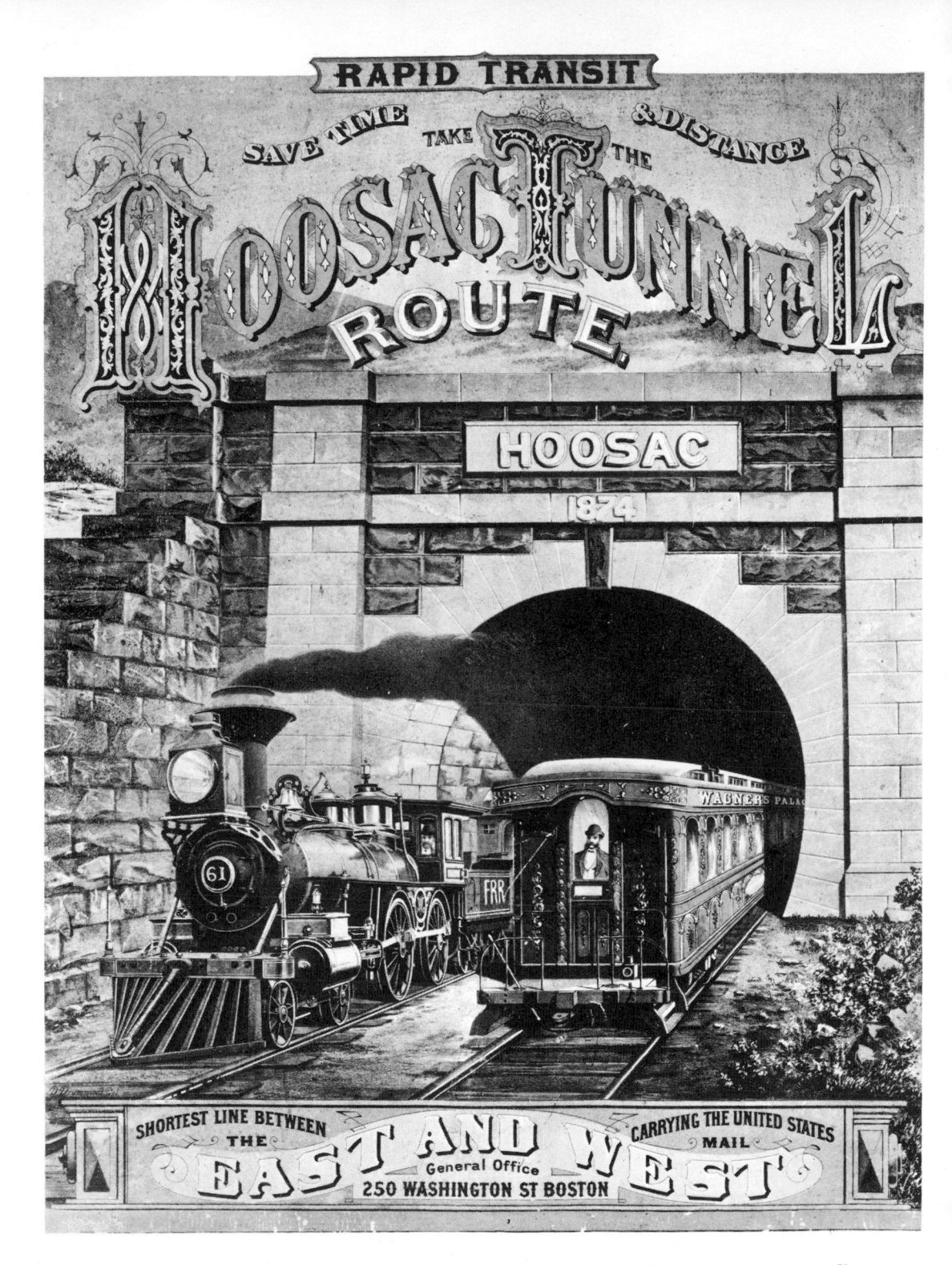

Advertising poster for the Hoosack Tunnel, Massachusetts. Drillers first went to work on it in 1851 and finished it in late 1875—almost twenty-five years later!
COVERDALE & COLPITTS COLLECTION, BROWN BROTHERS

Whistles and headlights, rails and crossties, sand domes and schedules—all helped to solve difficult railroading problems. Yet as the railroad builders pushed on, laying more and more track, they came to a problem of another kind and of quite another size. How could they get a railroad past a mountain?

There happened to be a mountain in southern Virginia with a huge cave running all the way through. The cave was a natural tunnel, high and wide, and open at both ends. Long ago the Southern Railway laid tracks through this gigantic hole in the rock, and trains use it to this day.

Other builders weren't so lucky. They had to dig their way through mountains. It took strong men to do this kind of work, and there were many heroes among them.

Most of the time, a man can't dig very far into the earth before he hits solid rock. Drillers have to bore holes in the rock in which they place explosives. Today, of course, powerful machines bore these holes very quickly. Years ago, drilling for the early railroad tunnels had to be done by hand.

The drillers worked in pairs. One man took a sharp steel rod called the *bit*, and held it against the rock. His partner gave the bit a mighty blow with a hammer, and small flakes of rock flew off.

Again and again the hammer came down on the steel. Each time, the bit went a little deeper into the rock. Between blows, the man who held the bit turned it slightly in the hole. When one bit got dull, he yanked it out and shoved a new one into the hole instantly, without interrupting the rhythm of the hammer blows.

Each member of the team knew and trusted the skill of the other. Swinging ten- or twelve-pound hammers with handles four feet long, men drove their steel bits down into the solid mountain rock.

John Henry was such a steel-driving man—a great Negro railroad worker who became a hero of songs and legends.

They said that John Henry could whip down steel with a hammer in *each* hand. They said he hit so hard and fast that the steel melted under the blows, and no one in all the land could keep up with him.

Then the steam drill came. One great puffing, hissing machine was supposed to do as much work as ten men. The legends say John Henry made a bet that he could beat the machine.

> Cap'n said to John Henry,
> "Gonna bring me a steam drill around.
> Take that steam drill out on the job,
> Gonna whop that steel on down."

> John Henry said to the Cap'n,
> "A man ain't nothing but a man.
> If I let your steam drill beat me down,
> I'll die with the hammer in my hand."

*The track of the famous Georgetown Loop in Colorado started in
the bottom of a canyon, wound around, climbed the hill, and finally
crossed over itself on a bridge.*
DENVER PUBLIC LIBRARY, WESTERN COLLECTION

That is part of the song about John Henry. Some
stories say that he won. Others say he died with the
hammer in his hand. Either way, he helped to send
the rails where they had to go—into tunnels through the
mountains.

Tunnels cost a great deal of money and in the beginning many of them were built only high enough and
wide enough for trains to squeeze through. Railroaders
called them *rat holes*. The first tunnel ever built in the
United States was a rat hole through the Allegheny
Mountains in Pennsylvania.

When the railroad builders got to the Rockies, they
faced a thousand miles of mountains. Not even a hundred John Henrys could drill a rat hole that long! Since
the rails couldn't go *through* the mountains, they would
have to go *over* them.

Laying rails uphill was a very difficult job. A train could not climb a slope that was too steep, and the track had to wind back and forth along mountainsides for many miles in order to climb a very short distance.

The steepness of the track is called its *grade*. If a train climbs one foot higher uphill in each hundred feet of track, the grade is 1 per cent. If it climbs three feet, the grade is 3 per cent. Even though that doesn't sound very steep, an engine that can pull a train up a 3 per cent grade has to be four times as strong as the engine that pulls it on level track.

Old-timers say that cowboys used to help western trains climb steep grades by lassoing the locomotive with their ropes. Then their horses would pull hard enough to give the extra power the engineer needed.

Once a circus train stalled in the Rocky Mountains because the locomotive couldn't haul it up a steep hill. At any moment another train, which hadn't been warned, would be starting down the hill. What could the engineer do?

The circus manager came to the rescue. He unloaded two of his elephants and had them push the train to the top.

Railroad builders did everything they could, of course, to make grades as gentle as possible. They avoided even shallow dips and filled small gullies with earth. When a gully was too wide or deep to fill, they built a trestle to span it. A trestle was a framework made of wood cleverly braced so that it could hold the weight of rails and heavy trains.

One railroad company had to build high trestles across a series of canyons in the mountains. The company always scheduled its trains to make this part of the trip at night because railroad men claimed that passengers would die of fright if they had to travel the route by daylight!

An excursion train crossing an iron viaduct. The view was spectacular!
NEW YORK PUBLIC LIBRARY

Trestles carried trains over dry canyons and small streams. What happened when a railroad came to a wide river?

It would cross as people did—sometimes by bridge, sometimes by ferry—and sometimes on the ice! Ferries on the Missouri River, for example, stopped when the water froze in winter. Then crossties and rails were laid on posts driven down into the ice. Trains ran over this temporary track until spring thaws came and the ferries began running again.

Sometimes a train would cross a river on a floating pontoon bridge. This could be a great adventure, especially if the crossing was like one in Texas where the river ran between two steep banks. The locomotive had to go very fast down one bank and across the pontoon bridge, getting up enough speed to climb the bank on the other side. When the train rushed onto the bridge, the pontoons bounced, the track swayed, and the cars lurched wildly. Passengers seldom wanted to make the trip a second time.

At one time an 800-foot suspension bridge spanned the gorge at Niagara Falls, between the United States and Canada. It had a lower deck for wagons and pedestrians. CANADIAN NATIONAL RAILWAYS

Although the passengers in this picture are admiring the view of Mt. Washington, most travelers were more timid, and the railroads usually scheduled the scary part of the trip for the evening hours, when the passengers would be unable to see how high up they really were. NEW YORK PUBLIC LIBRARY

The first bridge to be built across the Mississippi River rested on stone pillars set in the water, and the trains ran over a framework of iron and wood. The bridge was strong and handsome. People on both sides of the river held a great celebration when the Rock Island Railroad ran its first train over the bridge on April 22, 1856. Yet on that very day a group of men were planning to destroy the new bridge. Why?

To the boatmen who *ferried* freight across the river, the bridge seemed to be a terrible threat. If the trains began to carry all the freight, the boatmen would lose their jobs. Other men also feared the new bridge—

the men who owned the ships and barges carrying freight up and down the river. Suppose the fast-growing railroads took away their shipping business?

Some of these men had tried hard to keep the railroad from building the bridge in the first place. After it was opened, they kept on worrying and complaining. One day a riverboat named the *Effie Afton* rammed the bridge and caught fire. The bridge went up in flames, too.

Was it really an accident? The boat had been brand-new, and no one could explain why one of her paddle wheels had jammed just at that moment and made her hit the bridge. A stove tipped over at the same time, yet no one paid any attention to the fire until the boat was ablaze. Had the *Effie Afton* really been wrecked on purpose, to destroy the bridge?

Many people thought so, especially when the boat's owners claimed that the accident was the railroad's fault! After all, they said, if the railroad bridge hadn't been built, the *Effie Afton* wouldn't have hit it. The boat's owners demanded that the railroad pay for the damage. Furthermore, they wanted to prove in court that *any* bridge across the river was illegal because it would interfere with the rights of riverboat owners.

Abraham Lincoln was the lawyer for the Rock Island Railroad. He argued that the river belonged to everybody and that everybody had a right to cross it— by boat or in any other way. The court agreed, and he won his case.

What Lincoln saw here was not just the rights and wrongs involved in this one case. He was thinking of the future. The country was huge, and he believed it would be very rich and productive if its many separated areas could be linked and developed. Only railroads could do that job.

It was 1856 when Lincoln won the Rock Island Railroad case. Four years later he won the election for President of the United States. In those days the President did not take office until the March after his election. And so President-elect Lincoln stayed at home in Illinois until late in the winter of 1861. When he did start for Washington in February, his trip turned out to be a strange and exciting one.

On the night of February 23, 1861, a mysterious train waited on the Pennsylvania Railroad track at the edge of the city of Harrisburg. It was the shortest possible train—just a locomotive, a tender, and one passenger car. The locomotive, which stood chuffing gently, showed no light and the passenger car too was unlighted. Presently two very tall men boarded the car and sat down in the dark. One of them, armed with pistols and knives, was a friend of Abraham Lincoln. The other was Lincoln himself.

Still without lights, the train began to move, and then gathered speed over a clear track toward Philadelphia. No other trains were running between the two cities. They all had been ordered to stand by. Even the telegraph wires had been cut, so that no messages could be sent out of Harrisburg. In fact, only a handful of people knew about the darkened train and who was on it.

Earlier in the day, Abraham Lincoln had appeared at a public meeting and a dinner party in Harrisburg. Now he was riding away secretly in the night. Instead of the high, stiff black hat which would easily identify him, he carried a small soft felt hat to wear when he left the train.

What was behind all this mystery?

Lincoln's friends had learned that a group of men were plotting to assassinate him the next day, when his train went through Baltimore. His friends insisted that he must be smuggled into the Capital secretly and ahead of time.

Information about the plot had come first from Allan Pinkerton, a detective who worked for the railroads, guarding trains and, some said, spying on employees for the owners. At first Lincoln did not take Pinkerton's report seriously. Then he heard the story again from some regular policemen who were investigating threats of violence in Baltimore. The southerners who lived in that city hated the idea of a northern president who might put an end to slavery in the South. It was also known that a secret military group in Baltimore was preparing for war against the North.

The President and his advisers listened to all these reports. Lincoln still felt that he should go through Baltimore on schedule, because the new President must not appear to be a coward.

It would be worse, said his friends, to have a brave President but a dead one.

Lincoln protested, but in the end he agreed to make the secret trip by night.

The most careful plans had been laid. When Lincoln left the dinner party in Harrisburg, his friends hinted that he did not feel well and was going to bed early. It was possible that a newspaper reporter would call at his hotel and discover that Lincoln was not there. The newsman might telegraph the story to his paper, and the plotters would be warned. As an extra precaution, the telegraph wires were cut to keep any news from leaking out. Lincoln's train was scheduled to run without lights, straight through to the Pennsylvania Railroad station in Philadelphia.

At Philadelphia, Lincoln changed not only trains but also railroads. For the next part of his trip he was to ride in a sleeping car on the Philadelphia, Wilmington & Baltimore Railroad—the P W & B.

The Superintendent of the P W & B was waiting on the Pennsylvania Railroad platform with the detective Allan Pinkerton. They guided Lincoln and his friend to a waiting carriage. Pinkerton gave instructions to the driver, then climbed in after the others.

As the horses trotted briskly up one dark Philadelphia street and down another, Pinkerton explained that it would be half an hour before the P W & B train pulled out and he had decided it would be safer to spend this time riding around in the carriage. To avoid suspicion, he had told the driver they were looking for a friend.

At last the carriage drew up at the P W & B station. One of Pinkerton's helpers, a woman detective, was already there. She had bought a ticket for her "invalid brother"—Lincoln, of course—who was to be brought in through the rear door of the last car.

President-elect Lincoln boards secret train with his friend, Ward Hill Lamon, and detective Allan Pinkerton.
DRAWING BY LLOYD OSTENDORF

This 16-wheel, armor-plated car was specially built for President Lincoln, but he never used it. After his death, it became part of his funeral train. BETTMANN ARCHIVE

Just before the conductor called "All aboard," Lincoln and his friend settled down in the darkened rear car. Pinkerton and the woman detective sat close by.

So they traveled, tense and in silence, until the train stopped on the east side of Baltimore at half-past three in the morning. Minutes later the locomotive pulled away and left the passenger car standing at the station.

Presently Lincoln heard a commotion outside. Men were hitching a team of horses to the car. Then off they went, hauling the car along rails through an almost deserted street, toward another station on the west side of town.

This was the way trains always went through Baltimore. No wonder Lincoln's advisers had begged him to make the trip secretly and at night! Nothing could have been more dangerous than a slowly moving, horse-drawn car in a street filled with an angry crowd.

Lincoln's car crept across town to the Baltimore & Ohio Railroad station, and there it was coupled into another train. Finally the B & O locomotive got up steam and the train was on its way to Washington.

Lincoln made a sleepy joke or two, then dozed off.

By six o'clock in the morning the telegraph key in Harrisburg was clicking again, and a puzzled operator was taking down a message from Washington, D.C., that said: Plums arrived with nuts all right. When this strange telegram was decoded, it meant: Lincoln (plums) had arrived with his friend (nuts).

The railroaders had delivered their new President safely to the Capital.

A few weeks later, when the Civil War began, both North and South realized the true value of railroads. The South had many miles of track, but all the mills

President Lincoln was assassinated on April 14, 1865, and his coffin was carried aboard this funeral train. The train left from Washington, D.C., traveling slowly so that services could be held in each city along the way to Springfield, Illinois, where Lincoln was buried. The trip took almost two weeks.
CULVER PICTURES

The General. This famous Civil War locomotive was kidnapped by Union raiders and recaptured by Confederate troops. The engine is still in existence and has been exhibited at many fairs.
LOUISVILLE & NASHVILLE RAILROAD

Union troops destroying Confederate track in Atlanta, Georgia, during the Civil War.
CULVER PICTURES

for making rails and shops for building locomotives and cars were in the North. Whenever Yankee raiders destroyed a section of Rebel track, they tore up the rails, built bonfies, heated each rail till it was red hot, and bent it into a knot around a tree trunk. The South could replace the rails only by importing new ones from England. In this way the Union army deprived the Confederate army of its railroads.

When the Union army marched into the South, their supply trains were not far behind. Rails from northern factories were carried along and quickly laid. Railroads had much to do with the Union army's victory.

When the Civil War ended, in 1865, the South faced a giant task—the problem of rebuilding. In the five years of war much of the land had been devastated, homes and crops had been destroyed, and food was scarce.

To start rebuilding, the South had to get its trains rolling, and since most of the locomotives in the South had been wrecked or disabled, men turned once again to horses. They hitched their teams to railroad cars, and slowly trains began moving across the land. For a time some trains even ran on wooden rails until iron rails could be bought. Little by little men began to farm and trade and work again.

In the North and West, growth came like an explosion. As new factories sprang up and cities grew larger, railroading boomed. Everyone needed railroads.

During the war, trains had already begun to carry mail. The first signal lights had begun to operate. Sleeping cars had become more comfortable and the first dining car had appeared. Now, with the war ended, builders began to lay tracks furiously from city to city, from state to state, and finally from sea to sea.

Passengers on trains crossing the plains often shot buffalo for sport. So did some of the railroaders. CULVER PICTURES

6

"The railroads are coming!"

That was the news that spread through the western wilderness in the summer of 1865. Men and women traveling in covered wagons brought the word across the Great Plains. They had heard the whistles and had seen the rails being laid. The Union Pacific Railway company was laying track from eastern Nebraska toward the Rocky Mountains in the west. The Central Pacific Railroad company was building from the coast of California eastward over the High Sierra mountains. Someday, the two railroads would meet.

Cowboys on the ranges heard the exciting news. There was going to be a railroad across Kansas! Soon they could drive great herds of longhorns to Dodge City, and from there the cattle could travel to the Chicago market in cars.

The prairie Indians watched the iron monster roaring across the plains with fear in their hearts. They were afraid that the white man's iron horse was going to destroy their buffalo-hunting grounds. And it did. The railroad builders in Kansas needed tons of meat to feed the thousand men working on the tracks. They hired a young fellow named Bill Cody to supply steaks for the crews. He provided the crews lavishly—with buffalo steaks. In just one year Cody killed 4,280 buffalo. Railroaders made up a song about him:

> Buffalo Bill, Buffalo Bill!
> Never missed and never will.
> Always aims and shoots to kill
> And the company pays his buffalo bill.

Although there were many buffalo hunters, Bill Cody was the best known.

A former general in the Union army named Grenville Dodge was in charge of building the Union Pacific Railway from Nebraska to the Rockies. Dodge was experienced in the problems of moving men and materials. From the very beginning, he knew he wasn't going to have an easy time. Everything he needed had to come from the East. All equipment and supplies had to be shipped to the Missouri River by train, ferried across by boat, put aboard another train, and finally loaded into wagons which hauled supplies to a construction camp. Rails had to come all the way from Pennsylvania, wood for the ties from Minnesota. (No trees grew on the Great Plains.) Since there were no steam shovels or bulldozers or trucks in the 1860's, all the digging, carrying, pushing, and pulling had to be done by men with picks and shovels and wheelbarrows and mules.

The crews that Dodge hired often made a great

deal of trouble. Some of the men were adventurers and crooks. Others were restless soldiers who hadn't gone home after the Civil War. Many were Irish immigrants who had heard that the railroads needed workers. These Irishmen laid track, swung hammers, and drilled and blasted rock. A famous song about the drillers, or tarriers, says:

> Drill, ye tarriers, drill!
> Drill, ye tarriers, drill!
> Oh, it's work all day,
> No sugar in your tay,
> Workin' on the U. Pay Rail-way!

Workers with picks, shovels, hammers, and drills break a trail for the rails of the Central Pacific. SOUTHERN PACIFIC

The Union Pacific lays track through Indian territory as Indians watch. CULVER PICTURES

If there was no sugar for tea, at least there was buffalo meat. Hunters for the "U. Pay" (Union Pacific) killed all the buffalo the crews could eat, and more. Naturally this alarmed the Indians who knew that their source of food, clothing, and shelter would be destroyed.

The Indians feared for their land, too. Although they had made treaties with the United States government, the railroad builders often paid no attention to these agreements. If a builder wanted to take a chunk out of an Indian reservation, he did. The government, instead of enforcing the treaties, sent Federal troops to guard the building crews when the Indians tried to drive the invaders out.

The problems General Dodge found in Nebraska were nothing compared to the difficulties that faced the Central Pacific Railroad builders in California when they decided to lay tracks eastward, across the mountains. The job seemed so impossible that one of the men who first proposed the idea was nicknamed "Crazy Judah."

Who but a crazy man would even dream of a railroad in the Far West? In addition to the problems of building across the mountain ranges, there were no factories, no shops, and no mills in California. Where would a builder get rails, locomotives, and cars? From the east coast, of course—by sailing ship. Loaded with equipment, the ships went around Cape Horn at the tip of South America and north again to California—a voyage of 15,000 miles.

Then there was another huge problem—labor. The Far West was still a land of pioneers, of independent men who liked to work for themselves and not for a boss. Where could a builder in California find his workers?

Charles Crocker, who was in charge of the Central Pacific, had an idea. He had heard there were many

workers in China who needed jobs. Why not bring men as well as locomotives from a far-off place?

The news soon traveled across the Pacific Ocean: Crocker would pay good wages. More than five thousand Chinese made the long journey to California, hoping to send money home to their families.

These Chinese turned out to be excellent workers —orderly, peaceful, and dependable. Such men seldom appeared on the violent American frontier. Without them, the Central Pacific might not have been finished until years later.

The mountains in California rise up almost from the sea. To the railroad builder this meant that the rails would have to climb steadily, rising on trestles, bridges, and complicated grades.

In one canyon, for example, the builders suddenly came to a high cliff. A shelf for the rails had to be blasted out of the solid rock, straight across the cliff face. First, men loaded with tools and equipment made their way up to the top of the cliff. There they put together a kind of elevator—a giant basket that could be lowered and raised by ropes. Riding in the basket, Chinese workers went down, drilled holes in the rock, put explosives in the holes, and then gave the signal to be raised.

The men who held the ropes heaved and pulled to get the basket up before the explosion came. They did not always succeed. No one knows how many Chinese workers died in this way.

In winter, snow fell steadily in the high mountains, forming drifts sometimes a hundred feet deep. Great snow slides swept away whole sections of track and buried the men. Yet somehow the building went on, and the Chinese crews pushed the rails, mile by slow mile, steadily eastward.

At the same time the Union Pacific was pushing westward. And now a race began between the builders.

Chinese crews blast out a bed for the rails. They were skilled at using explosives. BETTMANN ARCHIVE

Sometimes it took as many as eight locomotives to ram a snowplow through snowdrifts in the mountains to clear the tracks.
SOUTHERN PACIFIC

The interior of a snowshed. In the High Sierra Mountains, miles of snowsheds were built to cover the tracks. Some of the workers and their families lived in the sheds. SOUTHERN PACIFIC

"Camp Victory," April 28, 1869, when Central Pacific workers won the tracklaying bet for their boss. The crew lived in dormitory cars like those on the right. SOUTHERN PACIFIC

Each claimed his crews could lay the most track in one day.

Crocker of the Central Pacific urged his men to work faster and faster. The crews on the Union Pacific speeded up, too. Men grew so skillful that just three swift blows of their big hammers drove in the heavy spikes that held down the rail. After a while the Irish crews on the Union Pacific were laying seven miles of track in a day. The Chinese workers on the Central Pacific did the same.

Working ahead of the men who laid the rails, other crews built the roadbeds. They hauled earth, sliced through hills, put up unbelievably high, spidery trestles across valleys. We can guess how hard their job was by some of the names they gave to places along the way: Devil's Slide, Devil's Gate, Devil's Gulch.

Steadily the crews from the east worked toward the crews from the west. Crocker, the Central Pacific boss, made a final bet with the boss of the Union Pacific. The Chinese workers, said Crocker, would lay ten miles of track in a day. They did, and no Union Pacific crew ever beat their record.

The Golden Spike ceremony, May 10, 1869. After the ceremony, someone pulled out the Golden Spike and put an ordinary one in its place. UNION PACIFIC RAILROAD MUSEUM COLLECTION

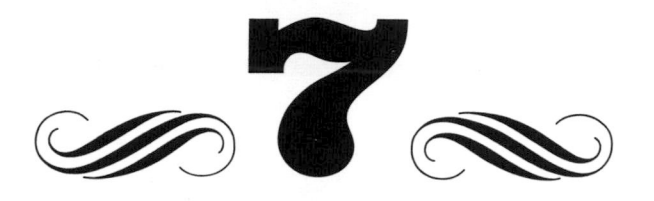

The Golden Spike

Closer and closer came the two rail lines. Now the Irish crews could see the Chinese crews working in the distance. The Chinese could hear the Irish singing as they hammered down the spikes.

The whole country was stirred by this race between the crews. The United States Congress was interested in it, too. Congress wanted to make sure that neither railroad company quit before the important job was finished. To encourage them, Congress had agreed to lend each company $48,000 for every mile of track it laid. Of course the owners of the Union Pacific wanted to get as much government money as possible. The owners of the Central Pacific were just as eager for it. That was one reason why each crew was urged to lay more miles of track than the other.

Telegraph lines were strung on poles as the Central Pacific laid its tracks to the East. SOUTHERN PACIFIC

At last the rails were close enough to join. But instead of joining, the Union Pacific men were ordered to keep right on laying track—parallel to the track that the Central Pacific was putting down. Congress had failed to name an exact place where the two roads should meet! Neither company wanted to give up any of the money by declaring that the race was over. To settle the matter, Congress acted quickly, fixing a definite point for the meeting of the rails.

May 10, 1869, was to be the great day. The place was a tiny settlement in the Utah wilderness called Promontory. Across the country people got ready to celebrate.

Of course, there had to be a ceremony to mark the opening day. Why not fasten down the very last section of track with spikes made of silver and gold? Better still, why not have important officials of the two railroads hammer these spikes into place?

That's the way it was done. Crew men came to the track ahead of time and made holes in the ties to be sure that the officials would drive the spikes in properly.

What a wild, noisy celebration it was! Bands played while the president of the Central Pacific got ready to hammer in the last Golden Spike. He swung and missed. The crowd cheered. The vice-president of the Union Pacific swung, and he missed, too. More cheers. Other officials had their turn, sometimes hitting, sometimes missing, until the spikes, both silver and gold, were hammered down.

Then slowly a Union Pacific train from the east and a Central Pacific train from the west chuffed toward each other. Their engines touched. Rails now reached from sea to sea. America had a transcontinental railway!

Towns with hotels and restaurants sprang up alongside the track as the railroad was built. Many of these towns disappeared as soon as the railroad workers had left.
UNION PACIFIC RAILROAD MUSEUM COLLECTION

The first railroad race had scarcely ended when another began. This time the contest was between the D & R G (Denver & Rio Grande Railroad) and the Atchison, Topeka and Santa Fe, usually called the Santa Fe.

Each of these two companies hoped to control all the railroad business in the Southwest. Both of them wanted to cross the mountains at a place called Raton Pass in New Mexico. Both wanted to run their trains through the Royal Gorge, a wild rocky canyon in Colorado. The Santa Fe won Raton Pass by a trick. One of its work crews was sent up in the dead of night to start laying out the road before the rival crew got there.

Then the D & R G captured the Royal Gorge and held it. There were skirmishes between the crews, and even a little shooting, before lawyers and judges finally decided that each road could keep what it had taken.

Other railroad builders laid thousands of miles of track in the same reckless spirit. It was a time of pushing ahead, of wanting and taking and accomplishing—often without regard for other people. Scoundrels and geniuses appeared, and often one man was both. Clever, ruthless bandits robbed the trains. Equally clever, ruthless railroad owners borrowed money from individuals or from banks, then kept it for themselves instead of buying new locomotives or building the good, level track they had promised to build. Some important railroad officials gave bribes to men in the government who then arranged the laws to suit the railroads. Trickery, scheming, and plotting were all a part of the building of American railroads.

But in spite of greedy and lawless men, the rails *were* laid. Before long our growing country had the great transportation system it needed—and most Americans rejoiced at every mile of new track.

In the battle for the Royal Gorge, the Denver & Rio Grande crew threatened to shoot the Santa Fe men.
DENVER PUBLIC LIBRARY, WESTERN COLLECTION

Railroads in 1870. The Civil War stopped their growth for a time, but railroad construction began again after the war. By 1870, the nation had 52,922 miles of rails. ASSOCIATION OF AMERICAN RAILROADS

Even in a blizzard, the brakeman had to race across the top of a moving freight train to set the hand brakes on each car. CULVER PICTURES

Dangerous Days

"Hurrah for the railroads!"

No wonder Americans felt like cheering. After May 10, 1869, a passenger could travel all the way from the Atlantic Ocean to the Pacific. But it was far from being a smooth trip—or even a safe one.

A traveler couldn't be sure, for example, that the engineer could stop his train once he got it started. Nobody had yet invented really good train brakes. Time after time dreadful accidents happened because there was no way to bring cars to a quick stop.

The train brakes that were being used worked too slowly, and they were undependable. When the engineer saw danger ahead, he gave three toots on the whistle. The whistle warned the brakemen, who then made a wild dash to set the hand brakes in each car. The men tried hard, but sometimes they couldn't get the job done in time.

George Westinghouse, a young inventor, set out to solve the problem. He knew the brake system had to work fast, and he was sure it had to be controlled by one man—the man who knew best when to use it—the engineer.

What kind of device would have enough power to tighten all the brakes in a whole train quickly and at almost the same moment? Westinghouse tried several ideas and discarded them. Then one day he found just what he was looking for. A story in a magazine told about a compressed air machine used for drilling a tunnel in Switzerland. The machine worked like this: First the air was pumped into a metal container. The pump squeezed or *compressed* a great deal of air into a small space. Then, when a valve in the container was opened, the packed-in air came out through a hose with tremendous force. It was this jet of compressed air that did the work.

If compressed air could push a drill, Westinghouse thought, surely it could push brakes up tight against wheels, tight enough to make the wheels stop turning. First he built a pump, run by the train's own engine. The pump compressed the air into a tank under the locomotive cab. Now when the engineer opened a valve in the tank, air shot out, ran through hoses that were strung along beneath the railroad cars, and clamped the brakes against the wheels.

Would the brakes work? A group of interested railroad officials let Westinghouse install his air brakes on one of their trains. To see whether the invention really worked, they came aboard for the trial run.

The train left the station and picked up speed. Suddenly, on the road that ran beside the track, a wagon driver turned his team toward the railway crossing ahead. The horses caught sight of the train, reared in

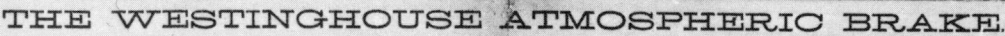

The original advertisement that George Westinghouse used in 1872 to explain his automatic air brakes. WESTINGHOUSE CORPORATION

fright, and threw the driver from the wagon. He came down hard on the rails—and didn't move.

The horrified engineer grabbed the brake valve and wrenched it open. The train stopped, just four feet from the man who lay unconscious across the track.

What a way to test an invention! Westinghouse was triumphant.

Then he began to have second thoughts. Suppose a leak had developed in the hose sometime before the engineer needed the brakes so desperately. The brakes wouldn't have worked. All the compressed air would have escaped through the hole in the hose. Air brakes were as dangerous as hand brakes—perhaps more so.

Westinghouse went back to the workshop and turned his original idea upside down. In his new brake system, the hose was always kept full of compressed air, but this time the air held the brakes *away from* the wheels. As long as the brakes were off, the train could run. If anything happened to the hose or the pump, the air pressure would suddenly stop and the brakes would slam against the wheels. The train would stop immediately, and the engineer would know that something was wrong.

George Westinghouse made a few more improvements in his invention. Then in 1872, when he felt satisfied with it, he put an advertisement in a railroad newspaper.

The advertisement did not exaggerate.

Now there really *was* an efficient way to stop a train. But did all the railroads in the United States hurry to equip all their trains with safety brakes? They did not. Fifteen years later only a few passenger trains had air brakes, and not one freight train used them.

The railroad companies argued that it would cost too much to equip their thousands of passenger and

freight cars with safety brakes. The old fashioned brakes cost lives, of course, but the passenger just had to take a chance that he would be one of the lucky survivors in an accident. Railroads were in business to make money, after all, not to coddle their passengers and crews.

Good brakes weren't the only safety device that railroads lacked. There was no danger-free way of joining—or coupling—the cars to make up the train.

On the earliest trains, a length of chain hitched one car to the next. Later, special devices were invented, and the one that most railroads finally adopted was a distant cousin of the chain. It was called the link-and-pin coupler. The link really did resemble the link of a great chain, and it connected each car with the next one. A removable pin at each end of the link held it in place. These pins were long spikes with rounded tops, and they had to be put in or taken out by hand when cars were coupled or uncoupled.

If the train gave a sudden jerk while a brakeman was still working with a pin, his fingers might be cut off. Sometimes, to release a pin, he had to step in between the moving cars at the risk of being crushed to death.

In Kansas City alone, four men were either killed or badly hurt in such link-and-pin accidents every week.

Could these accidents be prevented? Eli Janney, an inventor, thought so. While George Westinghouse was experimenting with safety brakes, Janney designed a coupler that linked cars automatically.

Imagine a right hand with cupped fingers sticking out at the back of a railroad car. On the next car, there is a cupped left hand. When the two slide past each other, the fingers automatically grip in a tight lock. To release the grip, a brakeman pulls a lever on the side of the car. That's the way an automatic coupler works.

A brakeman risked life and limb every time he stepped between two cars to join or separate the old link-and-pin coupler.
LOUISVILLE & NASHVILLE RAILROAD

The automatic coupler was an efficient and safe way to join cars together. It is still in use today. ASSOCIATION OF AMERICAN RAILROADS

Even though Janney's coupler worked almost perfectly, the railroad owners said "too expensive!" Of course, nobody wanted link-and-pin accidents. Nobody wanted to see men hurt or killed. But at that time the railroad companies didn't feel they were responsible for the people who worked for them.

One man thought the companies were wrong. His name was Lorenzo Coffin, and he has a special place in the history of railroad safety. In the 1870's he rode around the country on trains and collected stories about brake and coupling accidents. Then he started a campaign to force the railroads to install safer equipment.

Sometimes Lorenzo Coffin seemed to be more than just one man. He was everywhere. He talked to everybody. He badgered officials, legislators, and congressmen, urging them to act, and he made speeches and wrote articles. Few people in high places listened to him, but Coffin went on preaching safety.

Year after year the problem grew more urgent. There had been only 35,000 miles of track when the Civil War ended in 1865. By 1876, eleven years later, more than twice that many miles of track were in use. But travelers on even the best-run railroads were not truly safe.

Link-and-pin coupler

People in small towns along the track welcome a transcontinental train as it crosses the country. BETTMANN ARCHIVE

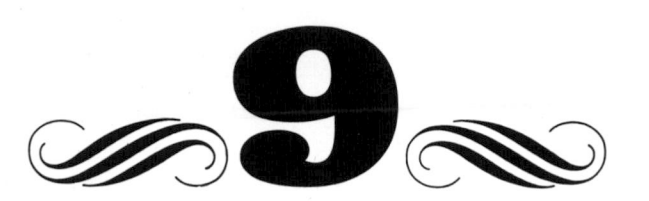

Speed Record

"Go it!" yelled the crowd standing beside the track. The engineer answered with a wave and a blast of the whistle. He was racing his train against time that day in June 1876.

This special train had left New York City, headed for San Francisco, with some famous actors and their friends on board. The trip usually took seven days, but just as a stunt, the actors wanted to cross the whole country in exactly half that time!

All along the way people gathered to watch the Special go by. It thundered over the Mississippi River bridge, across the prairie, on into the Rocky Mountains, making only a few stops. In Utah a journal box on one car began to smoke, but a bold railroader volunteered to fix it without a halt. He crept out onto the steps of the car, leaned down and poured oil into the journal box while the Special raced on.

At Reno, Nevada, the crowds lighted bonfires and set off cannon to cheer the train on its way. The passengers replied with bursts of fireworks from the rear platform.

Down from the mountains, into California, the Special was running a mile a minute. At every station throngs cheered the racing train. Thousands turned out to greet it in wild excitement when, just three and one-half days after it had left New York, the Special rolled to a stop in San Francisco.

Across the United States in three and one-half days! How was it done? It had taken several crews to run the train and set a transcontinental speed record. Once or twice only luck had kept the Special on the track. The rest of the time it was skill. The engineers knew just how to get the most power from their locomotives, and just how fast they dared to go around curves or down steep mountain grades.

The men who ran the Special were only a few of the growing number of railroaders who loved their jobs and did them well. They put in long hours, sometimes *more than twenty-four hours* at a stretch. They risked their lives, grumbled and laughed, and made the trains go.

Railroaders had good reason to grumble. Sometimes they got their wages on payday, sometimes not. Often they had to wait a month, even three months, to collect back pay. Worst of all, most trains still lacked safety equipment. Many lives were lost because automatic couplers and air brakes had not yet been installed. Work was so dangerous that insurance companies often refused to sell railroaders any insurance at all.

To take care of the men who had accidents, groups of railroaders began to form their own insurance companies. These groups, which were called Brotherhoods,

Maryland troops firing on the crowd during the Baltimore & Ohio Railroad Strike in 1877. CULVER PICTURES

grew bigger and stronger. At last they became the railroaders' trade unions.

Before the Brotherhoods turned into real unions, the men often had trouble settling disputes. In 1877 crews on the Baltimore & Ohio Railroad had been given several pay cuts, while the number of cars they had to take care of in each train had been doubled. Unfair, said the men! And dangerous! About forty brakemen and firemen decided to quit.

Other men joined them, and soon the strike spread to railroads all across the country. The strikers declared they would refuse to work until the railroad companies did something about their complaints. The companies

An engineer watches signals beside the track. A system of automatic block signals was invented by Westinghouse to warn the engineer that he must stop or to tell him to keep his train moving ahead.
CULVER PICTURES

answered by asking the government to send soldiers. Fighting broke out; people were killed, and at last the men had to end the strike.

For a while railroaders were discouraged. But the changes they wanted were on the way. The first improvements were made when railroad companies began equipping their trains with automatic couplers. Some companies also installed air brakes. Tireless old Lorenzo Coffin had kept up his demand for these two devices which would prevent so many accidents. At last, he and the railroad Brotherhoods began to see results. In 1893 Congress passed a law that required railroads to use safety equipment.

Almost immediately the astonished railroad owners made an interesting discovery: Safety was *profitable*, because trains could go faster with fewer wrecks.

Still there were problems about wages and working hours that had not been settled. The men who worked for the Pullman Company went on strike because of wage cuts in 1894, and many railroad union members joined them. Again people were killed, and the strike was lost.

The railroaders did not give up. After a while the companies did begin listening to the men, and again they made a discovery: Trains were better run when the crews had better wages and shorter hours. Many good working rules were adopted, and companies signed agreements with unions. Of course, struggles still went on—sometimes violent ones. For the most part, however, owners and unions fought less and talked more. Words settle most of their disagreements today.

One after another the railroad companies also kept on adopting new inventions to reduce danger. Today railroad people like to say that you are safer on a train than in your own home. They can prove it, too!

10

Time to Change

Trains were supposed to run on time—but before 1883 very few people could agree on what the correct time *was*. If several railroad lines used the same station, each company had its own clock installed. And every clock in the station might show a different time.

Time hadn't been important in the days when Americans traveled by horse-drawn wagon. The early settlers used the sun as their clock, and when the sun cast the shortest shadow, in the middle of the day, they knew it was noon. In towns that were big enough to have a jeweler, people set their clocks by his.

Of course, clocks set by the noon sun in one town did not agree with those in another town to the east or to the west. When the sun says it is noon in New York, it is a little before noon in Philadelphia, farther west. When it is noon by sun time in New York, it is not quite nine o'clock in the morning in San Francisco.

In the first years of railroading, time still didn't matter too much. Suppose a train ran between New York and Philadelphia. The engineer could easily remember that Philadelphia clocks were four minutes slow by New York time.

The problem became more complicated when trains began to go long distances. No engineer could remember all the changes he had to make in his watch. He might pull out of a station too soon, and passengers would miss the train. If he pulled out too late, another train might hit him from the rear.

Passengers too had trouble making connections between one railroad and another. For instance, Boston timetables would be made out according to Boston time, but at Hartford—a hundred miles west—the timetables would show Hartford time. There were about a hundred different railroad times in the United States in 1880.

It is hard to believe that people muddled along with this confusion about time for so many years, but they did. Some even took pride in it. In Kansas City, for example, there were several jewelers who claimed to have the right time, and they all disagreed. Those who liked one jeweler set their watches by his clock, and they wouldn't admit that any other could be correct.

As the railroads grew, it became clear that something had to be done to regulate time. Railroad officials finally met and set up what they called *time zones*. They divided the map of the country into four sections or zones, with boundary lines running north and south. The first section was the Eastern Standard Time Zone. The second was Central Standard, the third Mountain Standard, and the fourth Pacific Standard. Then it was agreed that all railroad clocks and watches within each zone would be set for the same hour. When the Eastern Standard clocks all said noon, all Central Standard

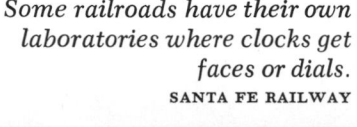

Engineers and conductors always compare their pocket watches before they start a trip.
RON ZIEL

Some railroads have their own laboratories where clocks get faces or dials.
SANTA FE RAILWAY

clocks would say eleven o'clock in the morning; Mountain Standard clocks, ten o'clock; and Pacific Standard clocks, nine o'clock. No matter what time a jeweler claimed it was, trains would run by Standard Time.

On November 18, 1883, at twelve o'clock noon in each zone, all railroad clocks and watches in the United States were changed to Standard Time. At last people could count on getting *where* they were supposed to be *when* they were supposed to be there.

If railroads could agree to having one kind of time, why couldn't they agree on one standard width for their tracks? In railroad talk, the distance between rails is called the *gauge*. In the early days, every railroad builder decided for himself what width or gauge to use.

He ordered tracks to be laid to whatever width he thought best. Some rails were five feet apart, some five feet four inches, some four feet nine inches, some four feet eight and one-half inches. The Erie Railroad had the widest gauge of all. Its rails were six feet apart.

For a long time no one worried about these differences. A man who wanted to ship some freight several hundred miles started it off on a car that belonged to one railroad company. Perhaps that company's tracks had a gauge of five feet (that is, the tracks were five feet apart). When the train came to the end of that company's line, men unloaded boxes, barrels, crates, and bales, and hauled them in a wagon across town to another station. There the freight was put aboard another company's railroad cars which ran on tracks of a different gauge. At the end of that line, freight was

The engineers of these locomotives waited until noon on November 18, 1883. Then they all yanked their whistle cords in a noisy salute to the adoption of Standard Time.
CHICAGO, BURLINGTON & QUINCY RAILROAD

transferred again, and so on until it reached its destination.

As the company grew, so did the amount of freight that had to be handled and shuffled from car to car. If the railroads could switch the freight *cars* instead of the freight, they could save much time and money. At last the railroad owners knew they must come to some agreement. They decided to use one another's tracks and cars. This meant that all tracks had to be of the same gauge. The owners of the large railroads agreed that it would be best to use the gauge of the Union Pacific and Central Pacific lines because their tracks reached across so much of the continent. This was to

Some freight trains are a mile or more long! This was one of many that carried Kansas wheat to market. SANTA FE RAILWAY

be the *standard gauge*. Railroads with other gauges would have to change.

What a job it was! Thousands of miles of rail had to be ripped up and relaid. The wheels on thousands of locomotives and cars had to be removed and adjusted to fit the standard track. Of course, this change could not be made in a single day, but it did come quickly. One Sunday in 1886, one railroad alone shifted 1800 miles of track to standard gauge.

Where did standard gauge—four feet eight and one-half inches—come from? Some people say that this odd measurement goes back two thousand years to ancient Rome.

A baby burro and railroaders in a mining town in the Rockies. This little narrow-gauge work car was used long ago by men who inspected or mended the tracks.
PHOTOGRAPHER: L. C. McCLURE, DENVER PUBLIC LIBRARY, WESTERN COLLECTION

Roman chariots had wheels that were set four feet eight and one-half inches apart. When Roman soldiers invaded the British Isles, they brought their chariots along, and the wheels made ruts that can still be seen in some places there today. After the Roman invaders left, English wagons continued to travel on the old roads, and wheels were made to fit the ruts. Later on train wheels were spaced the same as wagon wheels. This became English standard gauge.

Then American railroad builders bought some English locomotives and laid tracks to fit the wheels. In this way the old Roman gauge crossed the Atlantic Ocean and finally became standard gauge in the United States.

Standard gauge was not always best for trains that ran in the mountains. The builders of mountain railroads often chose to have rails two or three feet apart.

Little engines and cars were built to match. These narrow gauge trains could whip around sharp curves, and their midget locomotives pulled like giants up steep hills.

Narrow gauge railroads linked hundreds of mountain mining towns to the outside world, and hauled millions of dollars in gold and silver ore. But when the mines began to close, the little railroads went out of business. At last only one narrow gauge line was left in all of the Colorado Rockies. People who have a special affection for the small trains have not let the owners give this last one up. Today you can still ride in the tiny coaches, around sharp turns and over scary ledges, the locomotive whistle sounding sad and lonely in the canyons. For a few hours you can have the fun of imagining what travel was like in the days of the old Wild West.

Two engines pull a small train along a narrow shelf in a steep canyon in the Rocky Mountains in 1885.
LIBRARY, STATE HISTORICAL SOCIETY OF COLORADO

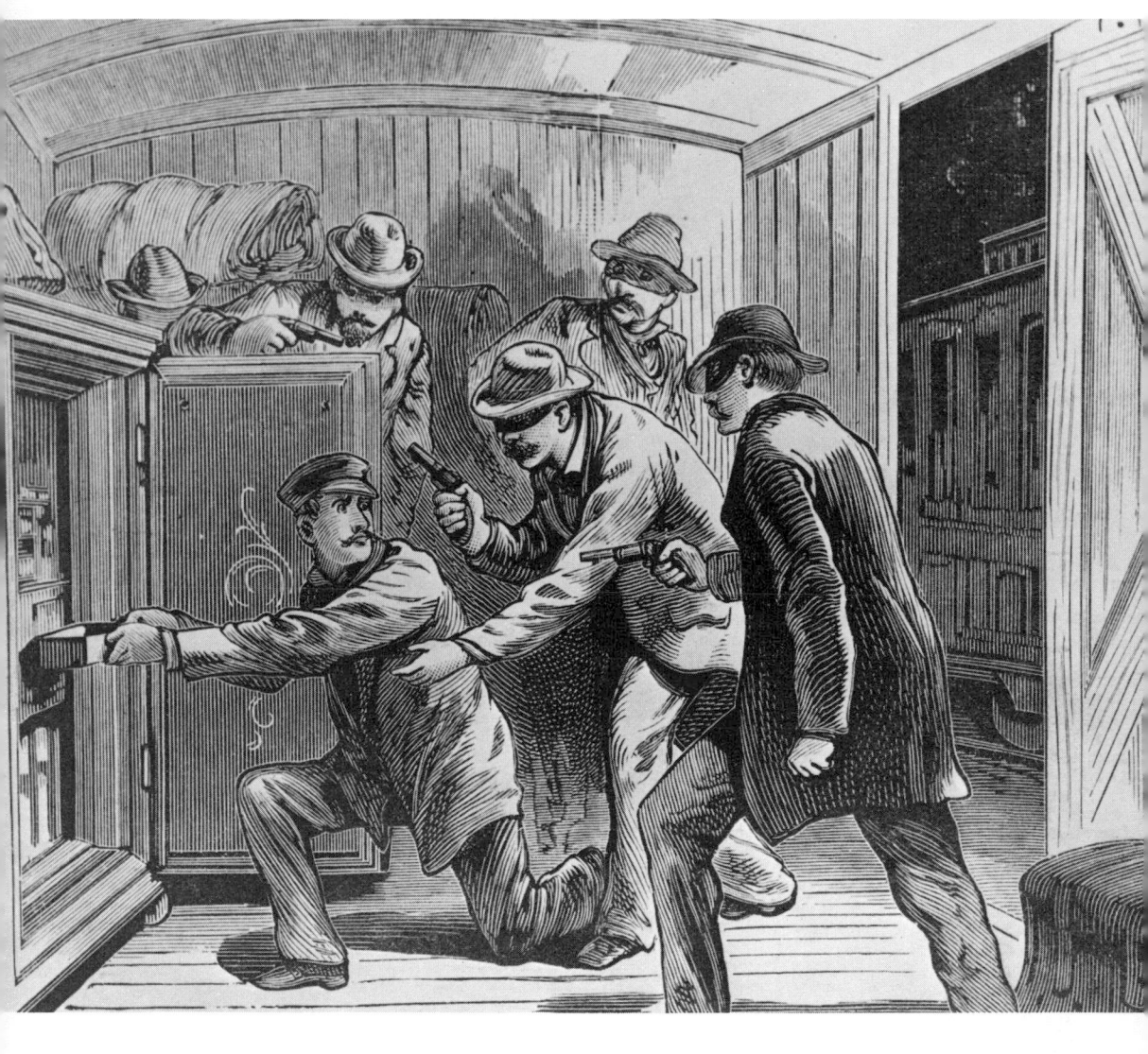

Hold-up! At gunpoint, bandits force the guard to open a safe full of valuables in a railway express car. CULVER PICTURES

Gold—$62,000 in gold coins! This was the treasure that came aboard a Southern Pacific train one day in 1884. Two armed men accompanied the heavy sacks of coins. Their car was not a regular Southern Pacific railroad car. It belonged to an independent company called Wells Fargo which made a business of hauling valuable freight all over the country. The armed guards were Wells Fargo men, and they were used to danger. They knew they might run into trouble on this trip, for they would be traveling across the wild Arizona Territory.

Ahead, in the city of Tucson, people waited eagerly for the Wells Fargo car to arrive. That $62,000 was payroll money for the railroaders, and for soldiers at an army post.

The station agent in Tucson looked at the clock. Just about now, he thought, the payroll train should be pulling into Pantano, a little town thirty miles to the east. Suddenly the telegraph key began to chatter. A message from Pantano: Bandits had just held up the Wells Fargo guards! Four bandits on horseback had snatched the sacks of gold and galloped off into the hills.

A few minutes later Tucson's sheriff, Bob Leatherwood, had gathered a posse of railroad workers and

soldiers who wanted to rescue their pay. Even before the train pulled into Tucson, they were riding east toward Pantano.

At a ranch in the foothills Leatherwood picked up the trail. He saw four sweat-stained, weary horses in a corral.

Yes, said the rancher, four tough characters had stopped there a little while ago and traded their tired horses for fresh ones.

"Which way did they go?" Sheriff Leatherwood asked.

"That way—headed for the hole in the ground."

"Hole in the ground?" the sheriff asked. "What hole?"

The rancher meant a cave in the side of a mountain not far away.

Bob Leatherwood and his posse rode on.

The trail across the yellow desert land led the men uphill. At last the sheriff located a dark break in the rocky mountainside. Four horses were tethered nearby.

One of the thousands of passages in Colossal Cave where train robbers might have hidden the sacks of gold coins.
LANDWEHR-MONKMEYER

Gold worth millions of dollars was shipped from this Wells Fargo office in Tombstone, near Tucson, Arizona. GUNNELL-MONKMEYER

Cautiously some of Leatherwood's men started into the cave's mouth. The next moment gunfire drove them out. A cave, the sheriff decided, made a bad kind of battleground. It was too dark inside to see the bandits, but the sheriff's men were perfect targets against the bright Arizona sky. The posse agreed there was no need to take chances. Although the men wanted their pay, they also wanted to live to spend it. Anyway, they decided, the bandits would soon get hungry enough to come out. Cheerfully the posse made camp near the mouth of the cave.

Next day when most of the railroaders went back to work, the sheriff and a few of the others stayed on. A week passed. Still no sign of the bandits. Had they lost their way inside the cave? Had they taken food supplies with them? The posse decided to wait it out.

A few days later, a cowboy rode by on his way home from a town called Wilcox on the other side of

Southern Pacific locomotives. Wells Fargo often coupled its express cars into trains powered by these huge locomotives. SOUTHERN PACIFIC

the mountain. Four men, he said, had appeared in Wilcox a short time ago with plenty of money to spend, boasting that they had played a great trick on Tucson's sheriff.

Leatherwood couldn't believe it. He had kept guard at the cave's entrance day and night. How could the bandits have escaped?

Yet the posse did find the bandits in Wilcox, and when the gun battle ended, three of them were dead. The fourth was captured—but only a small part of the money turned up.

Where was the rest of the gold?

The surviving bandit said he didn't know. He had stood guard at the cave entrance, ready to fire at the posse, while his friends hid the sacks of money somewhere in one of the underground passageways. They had promised to show him later exactly where the cache was, but now they were dead.

That was the story the bandit told at his trial, and he would not change one word of it. He refused to say how he and his friends had escaped the sheriff's guard at the cave. The trial ended, and he was sentenced to twenty-eight years in prison.

In the meantime, Wells Fargo detectives had begun to search the cave. For three months they looked

for the sacks of gold without success. The entire inside of the mountain seemed to be hollow. Vast corridors stretched on and on, with endless side passages. (Later visitors were to call it Colossal Cave—one of America's great natural wonders.)

The detectives finally left the cave, but Wells Fargo would not abandon the case. Twenty-eight years later a Wells Fargo man stood near the prison gate, waiting to take up the hunt. The train robber came out, went straight to Tucson—and gave his pursuer the slip!

Did he return to the cave? Did he pick up the remaining gold and escape with it? For a long time no one could say. The mystery went unsolved for years, and then one day some cave explorers discovered how the bandits had escaped the sheriff's posse. The cave had two entrances—one where the bandits had entered and another, about a quarter of a mile away, where they had sneaked out. The last secrets of the train robbers came to light when explorers found, in a remote passageway, a heap of old fashioned gold-coin sacks—empty. Each one bore the identifying Wells Fargo label.

Wells Fargo was only one of several famous express companies that handled shipments of money and other valuables. The first of these express services began long before the Civil War, when businessmen needed special messengers to carry important letters or packages from city to city. In those days the Federal post office system was not equipped to take care of such matters, and the express companies handled it. They had so much business that they built their own cars, which were coupled into railroad trains.

Messengers who guarded the express cars were employed by companies like Wells Fargo. Just the same, they considered themselves true railroaders—and indeed they were.

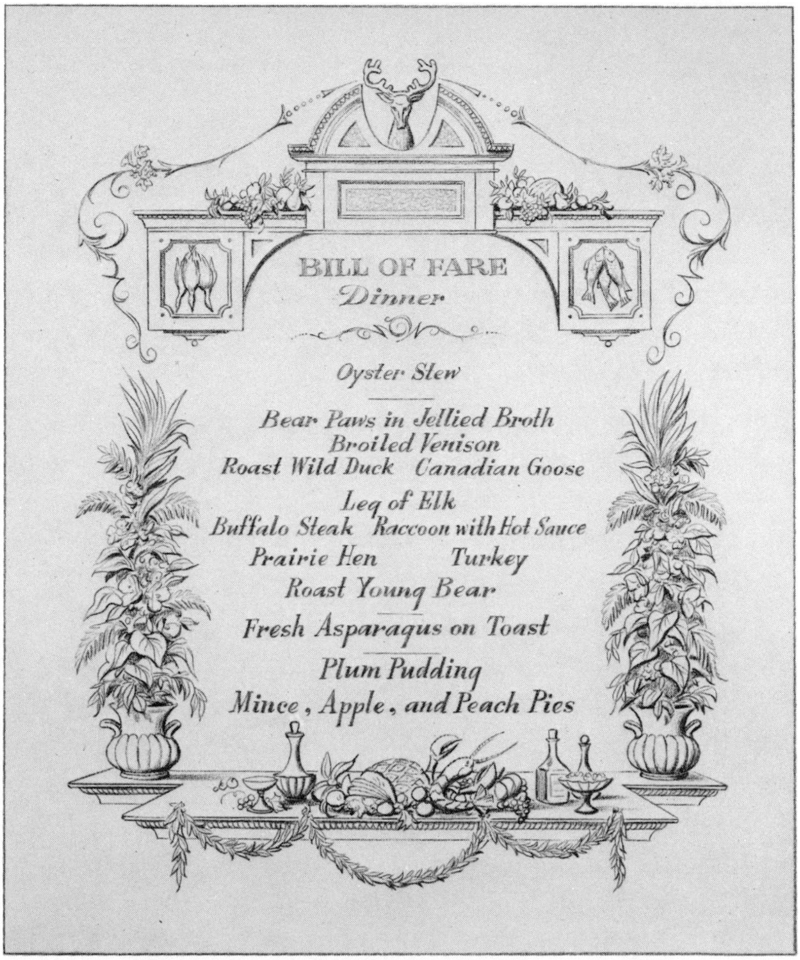

BILL OF FARE
Dinner

Oyster Stew

Bear Paws in Jellied Broth
Broiled Venison
Roast Wild Duck   Canadian Goose

Leg of Elk
Buffalo Steak   Raccoon with Hot Sauce
Prairie Hen   Turkey
Roast Young Bear

Fresh Asparagus on Toast

Plum Pudding
Mince, Apple, and Peach Pies

A typical menu for Christmas dinner in a Pullman dining car.

A luxurious dining room in a private railroad car. Sometimes the owner used his car as a home on rails.
BETTMANN ARCHIVE

12

Pullman and His Palace Cars

George Pullman was a man who liked comfort. He found so little of it when he first rode on trains that he decided to make a business of providing rest and refreshment for travelers. He started the Pullman Palace Car Company, and the name meant what it said. Pullman cars *were* like palaces—elegant, luxurious, fit for a king.

Royal meals were cooked and served in Pullman's dining cars. Usually dinner cost a dollar, but on Christmas Day it was free.

A good meal made traveling by train a pleasure, and so did a good night's sleep. But until George Pullman took an interest in railroad comfort, the words "sleeping car" were only a bad joke. Hard, triple-decker bunks ran along the sides of the car. Mattresses were dirty, which wasn't surprising because people went to

At night, a porter turned the seats in a Pullman car into comfortable upper and lower berths. BETTMANN ARCHIVE

bed with their shoes on. The bunks near the coal stoves got too hot, and the others were too cold. A passenger who wanted light was wise to bring his own candle.

By 1880 George Pullman had built sleepers that delighted overnight travelers. In the daytime a Pullman car had seats on either side of the aisle. At night the seats could be made into beds called berths, and above each of these lower berths an upper berth could be made by unfolding a kind of shelf that fitted into the wall.

Long green curtains hung from ceiling to floor on both sides of the Pullman car aisle. Each passenger

could fasten his set of curtains shut with huge buttons on the inside, and it was amazing how snug and safe he would feel when he buttoned himself in for the night.

A Pullman car had a dressing room at each end—one for men and one for women and children. Many people felt shy about using them and so they dressed and undressed in their berths. Ladies had to wriggle out of several sets of petticoats and stow them around in the small berth. Children wrestled with long underwear and high-buttoned shoes. But almost everybody agreed that a ride in a Pullman car was worth all the trouble.

As the railroads reached out over more and more of the country, they made some of their owners enor-

The men's dressing room in an early sleeping car. Water had to be pumped by hand into the wash bowl. BETTMANN ARCHIVE

Travelers enjoyed delicious meals cooked and served in Pullman's wonderful new dining cars. BETTMANN ARCHIVE

mously rich. These big railroad owners loved to show off their wealth, and George Pullman was happy to help them. He designed private railroad cars for them— even whole private trains with several cars—and filled them with the most elegant, expensive things he could find. He hired artists to paint pictures on the walls. There were velvet cushions, hand-carved furniture, organs to provide music. The water faucets in the bathrooms were made of solid gold.

One railroad owner traveled with his servants and his own doctor, and because he often needed milk for his stomach-aches, his own cow went along in the baggage car!

Even those who couldn't afford a car or a train of their own could travel in great style on trains called Limiteds. They stopped only at special stations, and there was an extra charge to ride in the fine parlor cars and the diners and the sleepers. One of these Limiteds

was named *The White Train*. It was painted entirely white, and trimmed with gold. Even the coal in the tender got a bath of whitewash before each trip began!

Only a few trains, of course, were as fancy as the Limiteds. Most passengers rode in ordinary cars called day coaches. For long trips they brought along well-filled lunch baskets, or they bought something from the vendors who went from car to car selling candy and fruit along with newspapers and magazines.

By the end of the 1890's the towns and cities of the United States were linked by 200,000 miles of track. Men traveled constantly on business, and for fun there were Sunday excursion trains that carried crowds of city people to the country for picnics. There were trains to the mountains and to the beach resorts. And if a girl were especially lucky, a young man might invite her to have a ride on the little railroad hand car.

Railroads had made a wilderness country into a thriving nation of enthusiastic train travelers. As the twentieth century began, people liked to say that any boy who had ambition could grow up to be President. Most boys, though, dreamed of becoming locomotive engineers—and thousands of them did.

Saying good-bye as a transcontinental train leaves the station. In the early 1800's, Wagner Sleeping Cars were almost as elegant as Pullman's cars. CULVER PICTURES

The engineer leans from his side of the cab and talks to the brakeman. The fireman's seat was on the other side. Both watched the track ahead. RON ZIEL

13

**The Man
at the Throttle**

Imagine what it was like to sit at the throttle of a great steam locomotive! You felt the power of the engine, and that power was yours to control. You were the engineer!

The engineer in his striped cap had a right to feel confident, for he knew his trade. The chances were that he had started out years before as a fireman. Then he had run a small switch engine that pushed cars around the freight yard. Next he graduated to slow freight locomotives, and finally to the command of a fast passenger train. By that time there was very little about locomotives that he did not understand.

An engineer also had to know and remember all the rules in the railroad rule book—and there were more than nine hundred of them! He knew the location of every curve and bridge, every sidetrack and signal on the division of the railroad where he worked. The big-

gest locomotive cabs held dozens of gauges, buttons, meters, levers, and other gadgets. These, too, the engineer mastered. So did the fireman, because he was the stand-in for the engineer in an emergency.

From the earliest days of railroading, engineers and firemen had a special devotion to their locomotives. People love engines, and the steam locomotive was among the best. When an engineer used his long-nosed oil can at every stop, it wasn't because a rule said he had to. He and the fireman took pride in smooth-running wheels.

The engineer was called the *driver* or the *runner* or sometimes the *hogger*, because a locomotive, especially a big one, was known as a *hog*.

No two engines were exactly the same. Every engineer got to know his own locomotive and learned how to coax it into running at its best. PHOTOGRAPHER: WILLIAM MOEDINGER, ENGINEER: JOHN J. BOWMAN

A fireman shoveling coal into the firebox. This firebox had butterfly doors that opened to either side.
PHOTOGRAPHER: A. F. SOZIO, RAILROAD MAGAZINE

The most famous driver of all was Casey Jones, a cheerful man who had both courage and skill. Casey drove hard. He fashioned his own whistle from six metal tubes, and blew it in his own special way. He had the bold, daring spirit that made a great engineer.

One night in April 1900, Casey was at the throttle of the *Cannonball,* a fast train that ran between Chicago and New Orleans. He had been delayed, but had made up the time and was running on schedule. Suddenly, on the dark track ahead, a stalled freight train loomed up. Its brakeman had not put out proper warning signals. The *Cannonball* plowed straight through the rear cars. Casey died in the wreck.

Steam locomotives stayed in the roundhouse when not in use. This roundhouse is now a museum.
BALTIMORE & OHIO TRANSPORTATION MUSEUM

Old engines inside the roundhouse-museum. The turntable in the center was used to turn engines so that each could enter its own stall for cleaning, oiling, and small repairs.
BALTIMORE & OHIO TRANSPORTATION MUSEUM

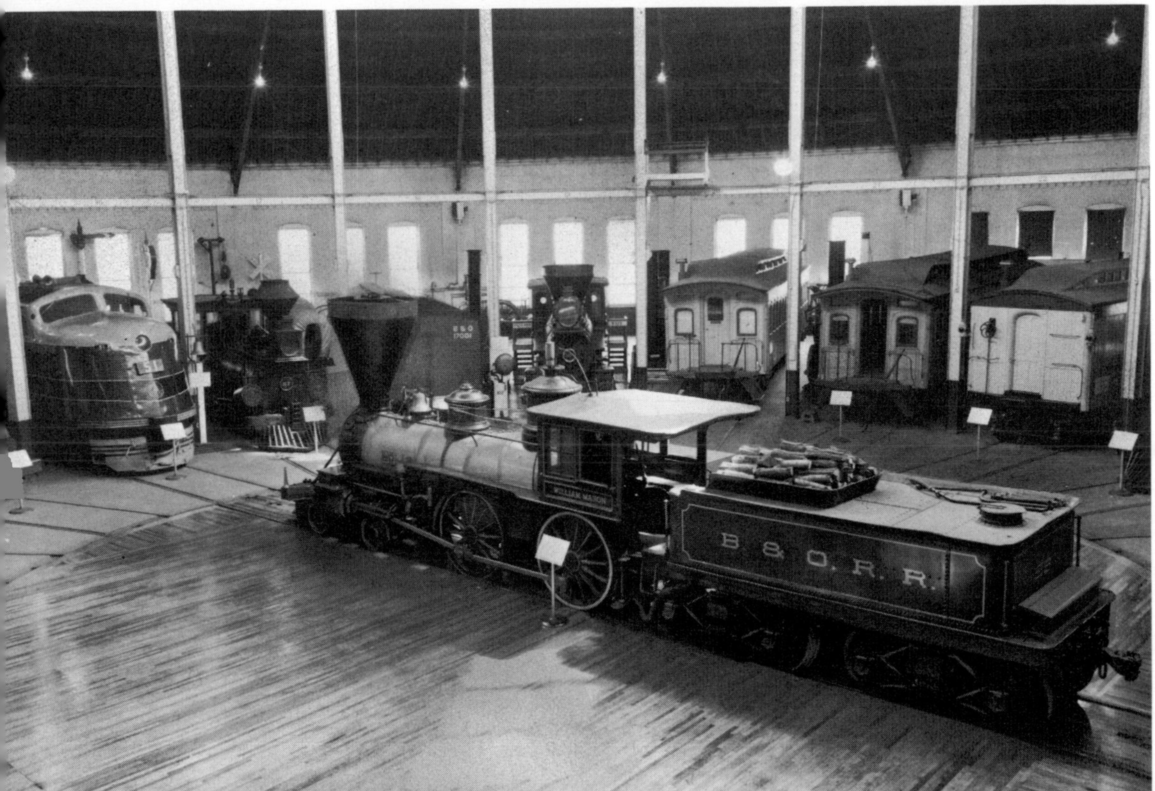

John Luther (Casey) Jones, in 1897. When the United States government put out a stamp honoring railroad workers, Casey's picture appeared on it. ILLINOIS CENTRAL RAILROAD

It was a song that made Casey famous. He had a friend, Wallace Saunders, a Negro roundhouse worker who liked to sing. After Casey's death, Saunders made up some verses about what had happened. He sang them as he worked. Others began to sing the song, too and even people who don't know much else about railroads know the story of Casey Jones.

When the United States government put out a stamp honoring railroad workers, Casey's picture appeared on it.

A steam locomotive of the 1850's standing beside a diesel of the 1950's.
ERIE RAILROAD

Casey Jones's locomotive had had ten wheels—six big ones (three on each side) and four small ones (two on each side). The big ones, called *drivers,* were turned by driving rods, and the rods themselves were moved by the pressure of steam. Long ago builders discovered that the drivers worked best if they carried a great deal of weight just above them. And so engines were designed with the main wheels under the boiler. Small wheels called *pilot wheels* were placed in front of the big wheels (drivers) on most engines. Many—but not Casey's—also had small wheels under the cab.

The more men learned about steam locomotives, the more combinations and arrangements they made with wheels. There were about forty different arrangements in the United States, and each type could be identified by a set of numbers. To name them properly start counting from the front and work back. Casey's engine was a 4–6–0, which meant four pilot wheels, six

*The engine in which Casey Jones rode to his death. It was a 4-6-0—
that is, it had four pilot wheels and six drivers.*
ILLINOIS CENTRAL RAILROAD

*The Governor was the largest locomotive built before 1884, the only
4-10-0 built for use on an American railroad.* SOUTHERN PACIFIC

drivers, and *no* wheels under the cab. A 2–10–2 had two pilot wheels, ten drivers, and two wheels under the cab. One of the biggest was the 2–10–10–2, with two sets of drivers—ten wheels in each set. It weighed more than a million pounds!

Everybody felt a shiver of excitement when one of the great steam locomotives pulled into a station and stood there panting after a fast run. This steady breathing sound came from the pump that compressed the air for the brakes. Occasionally the whole train seemed to give a deep sigh. That meant the engineer was testing the brake system to make sure it worked.

As the train pulled out again, the locomotive gave a few slow, mighty bellows. Then it settled into making a brisk choo-choo-choo-choo sound. This rhythmic chuffing came from the steam that turned the wheels and then escaped through an exhaust valve into the air. The exhaust on the very earliest locomotives made a terrible racket. Inventors tried to muffle it. As an experiment, one builder piped the exhaust steam into the smokestack. That did the trick. The racket changed into the agreeable sound which resulted in the nickname *choo-choo train*.

Steam locomotives were the only kind used on American railroads until 1895. That year the first electric engine went into service.

Electric engines had great power, and in places where there was plenty of electricity, they could be run more cheaply than steam locomotives. They were cleaner, too, because they did not pour out black smoke and cinders. But the electric current needed to run these engines wasn't always available.

In 1925, a strange-looking new locomotive began to push freight cars around and switch them from track to track at one big freight yard in New Jersey. This

Modern passenger diesel. *Diesel switch engine.* *Late steam locomotive.*
c. 1935

switch engine did not burn coal or wood. Instead, it burned fuel oil to generate its own electricity, and this electricity turned the wheels. Its huge motor was something like the motor in a diesel truck. It was, in fact, a diesel locomotive.

At first, this ugly duckling did not appeal to railroad people. They still had no idea what a remarkable engine it was. A diesel locomotive was cheaper to run than a steam locomotive. Since it burned fuel oil instead of coal, it was cleaner. It could make better time, partly because it went around curves about ten miles an hour faster than a steam locomotive.

Engine "999." DeWitt Clinton.
c. 1895   1831

A huge new diesel had plenty of power, too. If extra power was needed to haul a long train up a steep grade, a second or a third engine was added at the head end. These extra engines were not like the extra steam locomotives that helped to get trains uphill. A steam helper engine needed an engineer and a fireman, just as other locomotives did. A diesel helper did not need an extra crew. When the helper was joined to the main locomotive, one engineer could control the tremendous power of both engines.

Altogether a diesel was a very good engine, and railroad companies bought more and more of them.

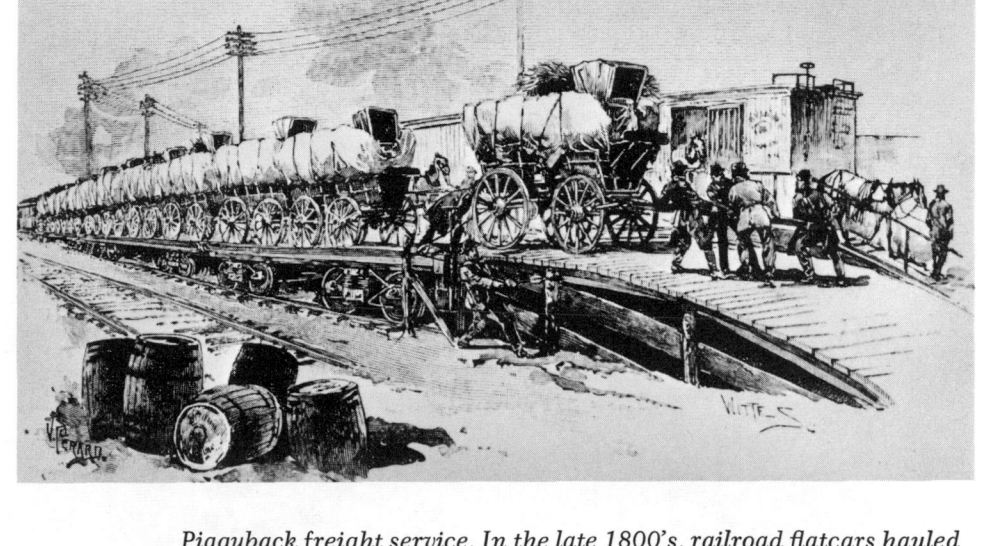

Piggyback freight service. In the late 1800's, railroad flatcars hauled farm wagons containing produce to market, just as today's trains haul loaded truck-trailers. BETTMANN ARCHIVE, ILLINOIS CENTRAL RAILROAD

TYPES OF FREIGHT CARS

Refrigerator car RAILROAD MAGAZINE

Covered hopper SEABOARD AIR LINE RAILROAD

Tank car RON ZIEL

Open jumbo hopper GREAT NORTHERN RAILWAY

One of the world's largest livestock cars which carries hogs, calves, or lambs.
NORTHERN PACIFIC RAILWAY

Then a surprising thing happened. The companies began to get angry letters about their fine new locomotives. People didn't like them! And why not? Because diesels didn't have whistles. Instead, they were equipped with horns that made a loud mooing noise which bothered everybody who loved the familiar, mournful sound of the old steam whistles.

At first the owners of railroads thought that people would get used to diesel horns, but the complaints kept coming in. Finally an expert was hired to solve the problem. He made a scientific study of steam whistles. Then he tried to invent a horn that would sound as if it were blown with steam instead of compressed air. He never did get exactly the same sound, but he came close enough so that many people were satisfied. Most diesels now have horns something like the one this expert invented.

By 1950 almost all the railroad companies were buying diesels. One by one the great steam locomotives disappeared. Railroad companies kept a few to use in emergencies. Some were taken to railroad museums, but most of them went to "graveyards"—junk yards where they rusted away. Movie companies bought two or three of the famous old engines and kept them to use in historical pictures. Other steam locomotives were sent into head-on collisions so that movie makers could film the wrecks.

A modern double-decker commuter train. Its locomotive can pull or push the coaches in either direction. CHICAGO & NORTH WESTERN RAILWAY

A dome car. Seated in the glass-enclosed dome, passengers can see all the scenery along the route. SANTA FE RAILWAY

CHICAGO, BURLINGTON & QUINCY RAILROAD, RAILROAD MAGAZINE

Each time a famous old steam locomotive was replaced by a new diesel, passengers flocked to the station for a last ride. They still loved the steam trains. They hated to see them go.

By 1960 only a few small companies still ran steam trains. Diesel locomotives had taken over. Without the steam engines, railroading would never be the same again.

Railroading was changing for another reason— fewer people were traveling by train. Every year, more passengers deserted the railroads because they preferred to drive or take a bus or plane.

By 1970 it was possible to drive an automobile over hardtop roads almost anywhere, even into the wild areas of deserts and mountains. But there were fewer places than ever that could be reached by railroad, and there were fewer and fewer passenger trains running on the rails. Today there are millions of children in this country who have never ridden on a train. Some have never seen one.

The Tokyo-Osaka, Super-Express train as it races past the highest mountain in Japan, Mount Fujiyama. JAPANESE NATIONAL RAILWAYS

15

Are trains going to disappear completely, along with dinosaurs and dodo birds?

Probably not. For we are beginning to find that we still need the trains. Automobiles and buses now crowd the highways to and from the cities. City streets are jammed with traffic, the air is poisoned by car fumes, and even air traffic is becoming a serious problem.

Railroads must again come to our rescue. We need crack express trains for travel between big cities. We need many new commuter trains that will take people quickly to and from work. Since a train can carry more passengers than a hundred automobiles can, there would be less traffic everywhere.

These new trains must be comfortable and convenient, and they must be *fast*. Inventors have begun to work on the passenger trains of the future. One kind

A high-speed aerotrain is tested in France. It moves on a cushion of air over a monorail. In the cockpit, the engineer pilots wear crash helmets and are strapped into their seats.

LONDON DAILY EXPRESS—PICTORIAL PARADE
A.F.P.—PICTORIAL PARADE

would resemble a train that is already operating in Japan. It has no locomotive. Instead, there are electric motors which turn every wheel in every car. The engineer sits in a cab at the front of the first car, and he uses levers to start, to brake, and to reverse the train. Once the train is under way, automatic controls take over the job. The engineer then has nothing to do—except in an emergency.

The Japanese train goes 125 miles an hour. A similar American train has been designed to go at least 160 miles an hour.

An American jet-powered train. During test runs, it set a record of 183.85 miles per hour. U.P.I.

A model for another kind of high-speed train has been tested, and it can go 200 miles an hour. It has no wheels. Just before it is ready to go, a pump in each car squirts compressed air downward through holes in the floor. The air raises the cars a few inches above the tracks, so that the train sits on a cushion of air. A jet engine pushes the train forward at tremendous speed. (Riding on the cushion of air, the cars are guided by smooth metal plates that press against the rails.)

Still another train would have small wheels for use only in stations at the beginning and end of a trip. To

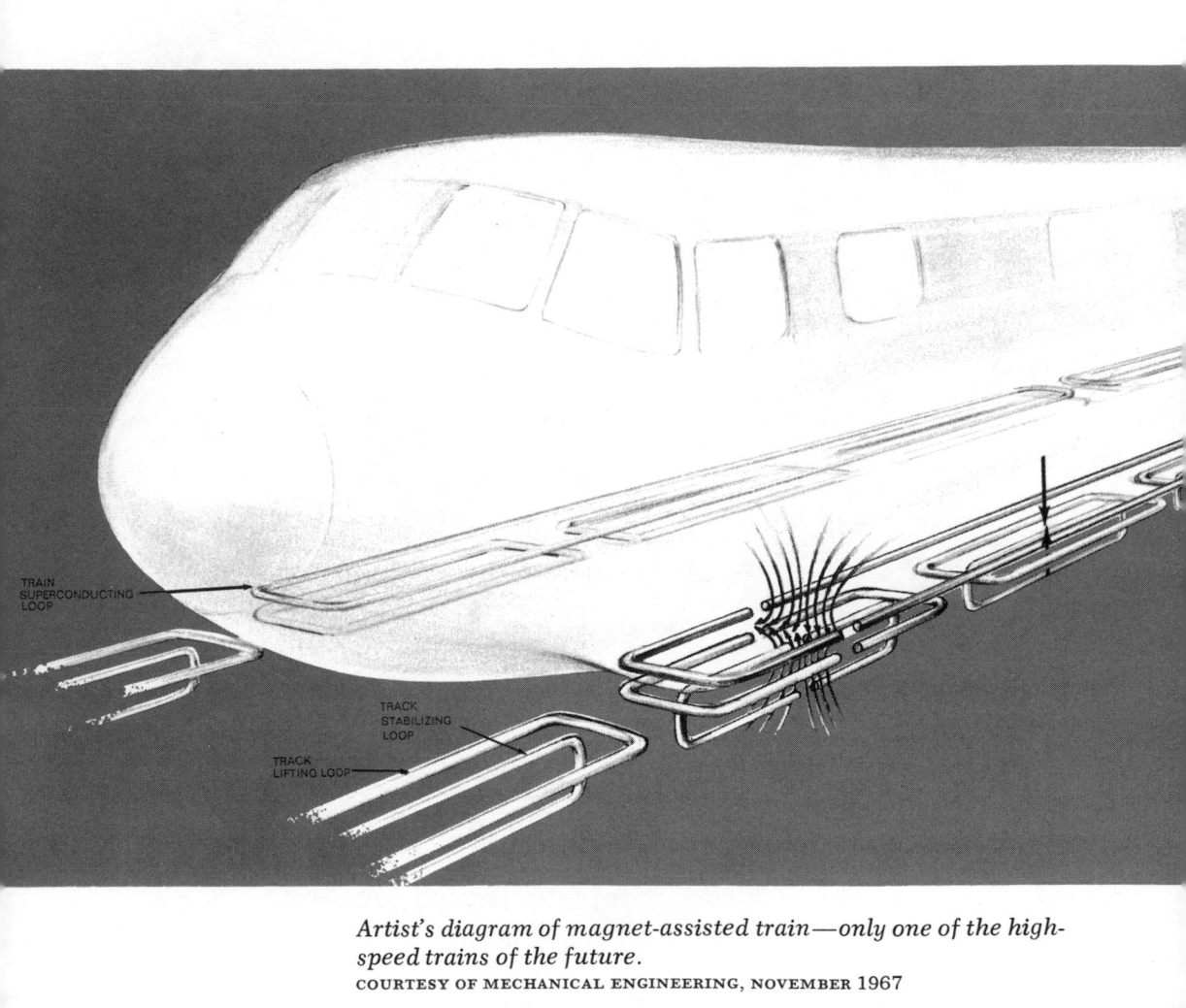

Artist's diagram of magnet-assisted train—only one of the high-speed trains of the future.
COURTESY OF MECHANICAL ENGINEERING, NOVEMBER 1967

TRAIN
SUPERCONDUCTING
LOOP

TRACK
STABILIZING
LOOP

TRACK
LIFTING LOOP

understand how this works, imagine a strong electric magnet in every car and another strong electric magnet in the track. These are arranged so that they do not attract, but repel each other. When electric current is turned on, the magnet in the tracks repels the magnets in the cars, and the whole train rises a few inches. Then a jet engine pushes it forward at about 300 miles an hour.

Some scientists believe that fumes from jet-powered trains would add too much pollution to the atmosphere. They have designed an engine that makes use of magnets to drive the train forward.

Even faster trains would run without either wheels or rails. They would slide along through smooth tubes underground at 500 miles an hour. The walls of the tube would be a guideway, so that there would be no need for wheels or rails. Air pumped into the tubes behind the train would push it forward, while a sort of gigantic "vacuum-cleaner" would pull out the air in front, increasing its speed. These superspeed trains probably would not have engineers but would be run by computers. Already a computer has run an experimental train in Canada.

It will be a long time, however, before engineers and steam trains disappear completely. Somewhere in the United States, there will always be an old-fashioned steam passenger train on which people can ride. Today, in more than half of our fifty states, there is at least one steam railroad still running—on weekends, sometimes on weekdays, too. Most of these little trains offer short rides, and some will take passengers on all-day trips.

Each year, thousands of people ride on the oldtime trains, listening to the sweet-sad sound of a real whistle. They envy the man at the throttle and relive the exciting days when power for his locomotive came from steam.

Index

D1649132